KU-313-110

Jessica Swale

BLUE STOCKINGS

NICK HERN BOOKS

London

www.nickhernbooks.co.uk

UNIVERSITY OF WINCHESTER
LIBRARY

A Nick Hern Book

Blue Stockings first published in Great Britain as a paperback original in 2013 by Nick Hern Books Limited, The Glasshouse, 49a Goldhawk Road, London W12 8QP

Blue Stockings copyright © 2013 Jessica Swale

Jessica Swale has asserted her right to be identified as the author of this work

Cover photo by Linda Carter of the 2012 RADA production of *Blue Stockings*, directed by Jessica Swale, designed by Philip Engleheart, featuring final-year BA Acting students, and supported by RADA production and design students
Cover design by Ned Hoste, 2H

Typeset by Nick Hern Books, London
Printed and bound in Great Britain by Mimeo Ltd, Huntingdon, Cambridgeshire PE29 6XX

A CIP catalogue record for this book is available from the British Library

ISBN   978 1 84842 329 9

CAUTION   All rights whatsoever in this play are strictly reserved. Requests to reproduce the text in whole or in part should be addressed to the publisher.

Amateur Performing Rights   Applications for performance, including readings and excerpts, by amateurs in the English language throughout the world should be addressed to the Performing Rights Manager, Nick Hern Books, The Glasshouse, 49a Goldhawk Road, London W12 8QP, *tel* +44 (0)20 8749 4953, *e-mail* info@nickhernbooks.co.uk, except as follows:

Australia: Dominie Drama, 8 Cross Street, Brookvale 2100, *fax* (2) 9938 8695, *e-mail* drama@dominie.com.au

New Zealand: Play Bureau, PO Box 420, New Plymouth, *fax* (6) 753 2150, *e-mail* play.bureau.nz@xtra.co.nz

South Africa: DALRO (pty) Ltd, PO Box 31627, 2017 Braamfontein, *tel* (11) 712 8000, *fax* (11) 403 9094, *e-mail* theatricals@dalro.co.za

United States and Canada: Macnaughton Lord Representation, see details below

Professional Performing Rights   Applications for performance by professionals in any medium and in any language throughout the world should be addressed to Macnaughton Lord Representation, 44 South Molton Street, London W1K 5RT, *fax* +44 (020) 7493 2444, *e-mail* helen@mlrep.com

No performance of any kind may be given unless a licence has been obtained. Applications should be made before rehearsals begin. Publication of this play does not necessarily indicate its availability for amateur performance.

MIX
Paper from responsible sources
FSC   FSC® C019549
www.fsc.org

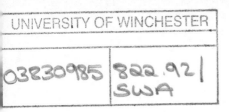

UNIVERSITY OF WINCHESTER

03830985 | 822.92 / SWA

Blue Stockings received its professional premiere at Shakespeare's Globe, London, on 24 August 2013, with the following cast:

LIBRARIAN/RADLEIGH/WAITER	Huss Garbiya
CAROLYN	Tala Gouveia
LLOYD/BILLY	Tom Lawrence
COLLINS/MR PECK	Christopher Logan
MAEVE	Molly Logan
MISS WELSH	Gabrielle Lloyd
MISS BLAKE	Sarah MacRae
MR BANKS	Fergal McElherron
MAUDSLEY/ANDERSON	Edward Peel
TESS	Ellie Piercy
MINNIE/WOMAN AT TABLE	Stephanie Racine
CELIA	Olivia Ross
RALPH	Joshua Silver
HOLMES	Perri Snowdon
EDWARDS	Matthew Tennyson
WILL	Luke Thompson
MISS BOTT/MRS LINDLEY	Hilary Tones
SUPERNUMERARIES	Robert Heard
	Kevin Leslie
MUSICIAN	Tom Lees
MUSICIAN	Richard Thomas

Director	John Dove
Designer	Michael Taylor
Composer	William Lyons
Musical Director	Phil Hopkins
Choreographer	Sian Williams
Globe Associate – Movement	Glynn MacDonald
Voice & Dialect	Martin McKellan
Fight Director	Terry King

Blue Stockings was performed in an earlier version at the
Jerwood Vanbrugh Theatre at the Royal Academy of Dramatic
Art, London, on 18 October 2012, with the following cast:

ELIZABETH WELSH	Sarah Kenny
CELIA WILLBOND	Rachel Redford
GERTIE MOFFAT	Verity Kirk
CAROLYN ADDISON	Ingrid Schiller
MAEVE SULLIVAN	Heather Long
MISS BLAKE/MINNIE	Jessie Buckley
MISS BEAUMONT/MISS BOTT	Ella Prince
LADY IN CAFÉ	
MR BANKS	William Alexander
CHARLIE MOFFAT/MR ANDERSON	Peter Hannah
RALPH MAYHEW/MR PECK	Tanmay Dhanaia
LLOYD/ PROF GODDARD	Frank Dillane
HOLMES/BILLY SULLIVAN/	Joss Porter
PROF RADLEIGH	
EDWARDS/DR MAUDSLEY	Harry Jardine
Director	Jessica Swale
Designer	Philip Englehart
Composer	Laura Forrest-Hay
Assistant Director	Lois Jeary

Note to the Players

In the mid-1800s, girls in England were lucky if they got an education at all. Some wealthy young women had governesses, some girls went to secondary school, but the curriculum was often limited to 'feminine subjects': needlework, art, maybe French if you were lucky, whilst the girls' brothers were learning algebra and translating Virgil by the age of eleven.

That began to change when Emily Davies, the pioneering educationalist, led a successful campaign to incorporate serious subjects and examinations into ladies education. Then, when she'd conquered the curriculum, she turned her attention to higher education. In 1869 she set up Britain's first residential college for women at Hitchin, Cambridgeshire. There, in a farmhouse twenty miles from Cambridge (considered to be a safe distance), the first women's university college was born. There were five students, taught by any lecturers that were willing to risk their reputations and cycle the forty-mile round trip to do so. But it was a beginning.

By 1896, the College had moved to Girton, a mere two miles up the hill from Cambridge (a schlep which was quickly christened 'the Girton grind'.) Yet, though the girls studied identical degrees to the men, when they'd finished their courses they were sent home empty-handed. When the men donned their caps and gowns for graduation, the women were denied their certificates. It was then that Girton's new Mistress, Elizabeth Welsh, alongside her staff and students, decided to begin the campaign to win the girls the right to graduate. And that is where the play begins.

As for the girls themselves, we tend to associate the Victorian era with stuffiness, modesty and proper manners. The girls at Girton were rebelling against that. Whilst they followed social rules and etiquette, in their passions and ambition they were stretching out of their Victorian corsets, pulling away from their demure mothers and moving rapidly into the twentieth century.

They are feisty, they are driven and they are the movers and shakers of their age.

As for the men, it would be easy to assume that those who condemn women's education with as much vitriol as Maudsley or Lloyd are heartless misogynists. That's simply not the case. These men speak the prevailing opinions of the time. They're not the devils of the piece; they genuinely believed that women's health and the future of Britain was at stake. I'd heartily recommend reading Maudsley's short book *Sex in Mind and in Education*, on which some of his text, and many of the sentiments of the play, are based, as a place to start.

Jessica Swale

Acknowledgements

Thank you to the National Theatre Studio for putting a pen in my hand; Bash at the Nash; Blanche McIntyre; Oxford School of Drama and my workshop actors; Ed Kemp and all at RADA; Lois Jeary, Laura Forrest-Hay and Phil Engleheart; Matt Applewhite and all at Nick Hern Books; Helen Mumby and all at MacNaughton Lord; Jane Robinson and the staff at the Girton archives; Dominic Dromgoole for taking a punt and having faith; to all at the Globe, especially our cast and crew; to the Swales, for listening to me read *all* the parts badly. To Lloyd Trott, a true mentor and inspiration, and to John Dove, whose generosity and wisdom has made this all possible. And finally, to Nell, Ella, Gugu and Michael, who have been the suspenders to this *Blue Stocking*. Thank you.

J.S.

For Malala Yousafzai
and all those who dedicate their lives to our education,
from the Girton pioneers to teachers, like my mother,
who inspire us all

Characters

*With the exception of Elizabeth Welsh and Tess, all parts can be
doubled. The play can be staged with approximately twelve
actors.*

Note on the Text

A forward slash (/) represents an interruption from the next speaker, to indicate where that actor should cut into the line.

Setting

It is 1896 at Girton College, Cambridge, home to Britain's first female university students.

This text went to press before the end of rehearsals and so may differ slightly from the play as performed.

ACT ONE

Prologue

September 1896. The first day of term at Cambridge University.

Smoke. Steam. Music. Train sounds. Dozens of men's legs in gowns hurry past on their way from the train to their Cambridge halls. Bustle, shouting. Then, through the smoke, four pairs of women's feet, daintily glad in lace-up boots, emerge and move towards us. As they come into the light these four WOMEN, *suitcases in hand, looking up, out over the audience, at Girton College. Blackout.*

Then DR MAUDSLEY *appears and addresses assembled male students* (*the audience*) *on his latest treatise,* Sex in Mind and in Education. *As he speaks,* MRS WELSH, *Principal of Girton, appears and takes in her female students* (*also the audience*) *on their first day of term.*

DR MAUDSLEY. Gentlemen. The Higher Education of Women. There are some women who choose to overlook their natural, maternal instincts in favour of academia. Literary women. Scientists. 'Blue stockings.' But the fact of the matter is this. Women cannot dispense with the physiological limitations of their sex, however hard they try. We have a finite amount of energy. A man who has tolled a field all day hasn't the capacity for mental taxation. Likewise, a woman who expends her energy exercising the brain does so at the expense of her vital organs. Women's nerve centres are fragile, pressure may weaken them, leaving them unfit for motherhood. In short, the higher education of women may be detrimental to their physiology, to the family, to the future of our society. Gentlemen, degrees for women…

MRS WELSH. Degrees for women.

DR MAUDSLEY. It's a dangerous idea.

MRS WELSH. What an idea.

DR MAUDSLEY. It may be a pity for women that they are born women, but in running the intellectual race, it's unlikely they will succeed, and perilous to even try.

MRS WELSH. Ladies. Welcome to Girton.

Scene One

The Laws of Motion

Outside, on the forecourt of Girton College. TESS *arrives looking self-conscious. She wears a makeshift bicycle outfit, large bloomers with stockings exposed. She looks down at her outfit.*

TESS. Right. Cripes.

> MAEVE *appears, wary, similarly dressed, non-committal.*

Oh, hello.

MAEVE. Hello.

TESS. Sleep well?

MAEVE. No.

TESS (*indicating her bloomers*). Any idea why we're 'festooned' in these?

MAEVE. No.

TESS. No, me neither. (*Pause.*) I think you're on my corridor. Are you in seven?

MAEVE. Yep.

TESS. Good. Well. We'll be neighbours then.

> MAEVE *says nothing.* TESS *offers* MAEVE *a smile, which is not returned.*

(*Quietly.*) Super.

> CELIA *appears, similarly dressed.*

CELIA. Science?

TESS. Yes. (*Indicating her outfit.*) Can't you tell?

CELIA. It's not usual, you know. We don't make a habit of dressing like this.

TESS. You're not a first year?

CELIA. No. I mean I am, sort of. I was. Are you Miss Moffat, or Sullivan – or –

TESS. Moffat. How did you know?

CELIA. There's just four of us in our study group.

TESS. So who's the / fourth?

CAROLYN *bounces over in the same outfit, interrupting.*

CAROLYN. Well I'm glad I'm not the only one that looks like a complete trollop. How do you do. Carolyn Cecilia Mouchette Addison.

TESS. Mouchette?

CAROLYN. Mother's from Paris. We lived there for a while, before we moved to Zurich.

CELIA. Actually, it's usual to wait till we're better acquainted before we use first names.

CAROLYN. Why? We're all going to be holed up together, aren't we? Might as well start as we mean to go on. Carolyn.

Pause.

TESS. I'm Tess.

CELIA. Alright. Celia.

MAEVE. Maeve. Sullivan.

CAROLYN. Charmed. Celia rescued me yesterday. Found me halfway up the stairs, wedged between my gargantuan trunk and the ceiling. Spiral staircases aren't designed for women of the world. Achilles almost had a fit.

TESS. Who's Achilles?

CAROLYN. My travelling companion. He's Greek. He's a wolfhound. He's fine now, he's dozing off on my bed.

CELIA. You know you're not allowed pets! If Mrs / Welsh finds out –

CAROLYN. She won't.

CELIA. But / honestly, if she –

MR BANKS *appears*.

MR BANKS. Ladies. Morning! My good wife will be thrilled that her spare pantaloons are serving the cause of scientific endeavour. Shall we begin?

CELIA. Mr Banks, may we ask why we're wearing bloomers?

TESS. Underwear!

MR BANKS. Follow me. You can do without those books for a start.

TESS. But we need them!

MR BANKS. You want to study the world, don't you? Not print on paper. Why do the leaves change colour? How does the hinge open the gate? Why, when I step, do I not float off into the ether?

CAROLYN. Because you're not a fairy?

MR BANKS. No.

CELIA. Because of gravitational force.

MR BANKS. Welcome back, Willbond. So, do fairies exist?

TESS. Of course not.

MR BANKS. Are you sure?

TESS. Perfectly sure.

MR BANKS. But can you prove it? Where's the evidence? 'Judge a man by his questions not by his answers.'

CELIA. Rousseau?

MR BANKS. Right country, wrong man.

CAROLYN. Napoleon?

MR BANKS. No.

> *Throughout* MAEVE *remains quite detached, giving her answers with slicing precision.*

MAEVE. Pierre-Marc-Gaston. Paris, 1808.

MR BANKS. Name?

MAEVE. Miss Sullivan, sir.

MR BANKS. To question is the hallmark of any worthy philosopher. 'The fool doth think that he is wise, but the wise man knows himself to be a fool.' Shakespeare, *The Taming of the Shrew.*

TESS. Sir, it's *As You Like It.* It's Touchstone.

MAEVE. Act Five, Scene One.

MR BANKS. Slow, but correct. Now. You are about to experience a miracle of modern invention. Wait there.

> *He goes off.*

CAROLYN. What's he doing?

TESS. Apparently he's an 'eccentric'.

CAROLYN. How do you know?

TESS. My friend Will said. He's at King's.

CAROLYN. At King's? A scholar? Are you and he…?

TESS. Oh no, we're just friends.

> CELIA *is watching* MR BANKS *wrestle with something, off.*

CELIA. What in God's / name –

TESS. Oh Lord!

> MR BANKS *emerges on a bicycle. All four* WOMEN *step back in trepidation.*

CAROLYN. A bicycle!

CELIA. I hope he doesn't expect us to / sit on it.

MR BANKS. A marvel, a miracle of modern engineering. Have a look.

CELIA *and* MAEVE *hang back.* TESS *is a little braver,* CAROLYN *more so.*

Come on. Come on!

They edge closer.

Now, what is this?

CAROLYN. The wheel, of course.

MR BANKS. It's not merely a wheel, miss.

CAROLYN. Addison. Carolyn.

MR BANKS. It's the life source. Without wheels, it's just a cumbersome chair. But with them, you can glide! The Mesopotamians invented the wheel to help them in battle.

CAROLYN. They didn't ride on bicycles!

MR BANKS. No, they rode chariots. Now, you.

TESS. Miss Moffat, sir.

MR BANKS. On you get.

TESS *isn't keen.*

TESS. I couldn't possibly.

MR BANKS. I thought you wanted to be a scientist.

CAROLYN. Go on, Tess.

CELIA. Go on.

TESS. Alright. Turn around please.

MR BANKS. As you wish.

MR BANKS *turns away.*

TESS. How do I get on?

CAROLYN. Just sling your leg over.

TESS. Girls don't 'sling'!

CAROLYN. Here, we'll help you.

CAROLYN and CELIA help TESS assemble herself on the bicycle. She starts slipping and yelps, causing MR BANKS to turn around.

TESS. Don't look, for Christ's sake!

MR BANKS. I'm sorry.

He turns away again. The WOMEN grab her and she reassembles herself.

TESS. Alright. You can turn round now.

He turns to the WOMEN.

MR BANKS. Now, observe her demonstration of Isaac Newton's theory of mechanics.

TESS. But I'm not doing anything.

MR BANKS. That's the first law of motion. That an object will continue in its state of rest, known as –

CAROLYN. Inertia.

MR BANKS. Inertia, or at its constant speed, until it's affected by an outside force. In other words, Moffat's not going anywhere unless she applies some energy. If you could oblige.

TESS. How?

MR BANKS. Place your foot on the pedal and push. Go on then, exert yourself!

TESS. Sir, I don't think it's ladylike to exert yourself.

MR BANKS. You're not ladies now, Moffat, you're scientists!

TESS. Yes, sir!

MR BANKS supports TESS as she begins to move.

MR BANKS. Better. Now, watch how the wheel rotates. A sublime demonstration of Newton's second law. Which is, Sullivan?

MAEVE. Acceleration of an object is directly proportional to the net force acting upon it.

MR BANKS. And force is?

MAEVE. The product of mass and acceleration.

MR BANKS. So the harder she pedals –

CELIA. The greater the force –

CAROLYN. And the quicker she accelerates.

MR BANKS. Now, if she were to ride to Midsummer Common, she might take a quarter of an hour, provided she's not distracted by the cows. Or the rowers.

TESS. Sir!

MR BANKS. How far is it?

CELIA. Two miles?

TESS. Blimey!

MR BANKS. And the equation for speed is –

TESS. Distance divided by time.

CAROLYN. One mile every seven and a half minutes.

TESS. Eight miles in an hour! Woo!

CAROLYN. I had a bicycle when we lived in Athens.

CELIA. Is there anywhere you haven't lived?

CAROLYN. Nope.

MR BANKS *lets go of the bike and* TESS *cycles alone.*

MR BANKS. Now, Moffat, you're off! And, with a grasp of the basic laws of motion, you can predict the movement of any object through space, from the turning of a wheel to the trajectory of the planets. It's tremendous. Go on. Faster. Faster! How does it feel?

TESS (*cycling off*). Like flying!

When she is out of sight, there is an almighty crash and a yell. MR BANKS *turns to the* WOMEN.

MR BANKS. Magnificent!

Scene Two

Sightseeing

Four MEN *stand and look out into the distance.* HOLMES, LLOYD, EDWARDS *and* WILL BENNETT.

EDWARDS. Right there! I saw it, plain as day, I swear to God.

They all look.

LLOYD. You don't believe in God.

EDWARDS. I know what I saw.

HOLMES. Bennett?

WILL *shrugs. He probably saw her… he probably recognised her.* RALPH *approaches.*

RALPH. Fellas.

HOLMES. Mayhew! You'll never guess what Edwards says he saw.

RALPH. You saw it too? A woman on a bicycle –

EDWARDS. Riding up the hill! Thank you!

RALPH. With a leg on each side.

EDWARDS. Sitting… astride.

LLOYD. Jesus. Here?

Silence.

HOLMES. In Cambridge.

Silence.

RALPH. I thought they weren't allowed to.

HOLMES. They're not.

Silence.

RALPH. She was going at quite a lick actually.

RALPH *smiles.* LLOYD *gives him a look of disbelief.*

Scene Three

The Happiness Equation

In MISS BLAKE*'s classroom. As they're assembling…*

MISS BLAKE. Well, how are you feeling? Full of the joys of youth?

ALL. Yes, ma'am.

MISS BLAKE. Happy to be here?

TESS. Yes, ma'am.

MISS BLAKE. Why?

TESS. Sorry, ma'am?

MISS BLAKE. Why does the being here in my class make you happy?

TESS. I've not studied moral science before.

MISS BLAKE. So happiness is knowledge, is it? Who said that?

CAROLYN. Socrates.

CELIA. How do you know that?

TESS. Athens.

CAROLYN. Yep. Greek restaurant. Inscribed on a plate on the wall.

MISS BLAKE. Maybe we should aim for a little more detail. So, is Socrates right? Is happiness knowledge? And if it is, why aren't Girton's doors being trampled down by women desperate for a piece of it? Miss Moffat?

TESS. Ma'am?

MISS BLAKE. Come on. Convince us – (*Having an idea.*) convince this 'parliament' that learning is your lifeblood.

TESS. You want my opinion?

MISS BLAKE. I've heard you can ride a bicycle. What's stopping you?

MISS BLAKE *sits and* TESS *takes her place.*

TESS. Alright! Well –

MISS BLAKE. Hesitation.

TESS. 'Knowledge is the wing wherewith we fly to heaven.' Shakespeare.

MISS BLAKE. Too slow. I was bored. Members of Parliament are supposed to be quick thinkers. Someone else.

CAROLYN. A monk once told me –

CELIA. Here we go.

CAROLYN. In Shanghai, I was told that he who knows himself is happy. Lao Tsu.

MISS BLAKE. And do you know yourself?

CAROLYN. Yes, ma'am.

MISS BLAKE. How very sure you are.

CELIA. Ma'am, Francis Bacon said happiness is power.

MISS BLAKE. Well if that's true, Queen Victoria should be the happiest woman in England.

TESS. She's hardly a ray of sunshine.

CAROLYN. Not with a dress sense like that.

MISS BLAKE. Valid point.

CELIA. Ma'am, the only thing that made Victoria happy was love.

MISS BLAKE. Ah, love! Of course. Happiness is love, is it? But what if you had to choose? Between love and knowledge. Which would you choose? A doting husband or a life of intellectual fire… and you're perfectly alone? Go on. Miss Moffat?

TESS. I – I wouldn't want to choose.

MISS BLAKE. Well I had to. (*Pause.*) Go on. Choose.

Pause.

TESS. I don't think I could.

CAROLYN *steps in with some trepidation.*

CAROLYN. Most women would choose a home life and a
family.

MISS BLAKE. But you're not most women.

TESS. No! And it wouldn't be enough… sitting around
arranging flowers if you don't know anything about the
flower, the miracle of its growth or why it exists!

CELIA. Ma'am, what if happiness is a simple life? Country air,
orchards, Scotch broth.

CAROLYN. How would an orchard make you happy?

MISS BLAKE. It would if you were Isaac Newton.

The WOMEN *might laugh at her joke.*

Miss Willbond, you're a cynic.

CELIA. I'm not, ma'am.

MISS BLAKE. Oh, don't be insulted, it's valuable
philosophical position. Diogenes was the first. He believed in
a life lived according to nature, and he lived by his words,
preaching to passers-by from a bathtub on the streets of
Athens –

CELIA. With no clothes on?

MISS BLAKE. He didn't believe in material things.

The WOMEN *find her wit funny.*

CAROLYN. But it's not true, is it.

MISS BLAKE. What isn't?

CAROLYN. 'The simple life.' It's just sentimental puff that's
said to make lower-class people feel better.

TESS. You can't say that.

CAROLYN. Oh come on. Who doesn't want material things?
No one wants to live like a factory worker in some

backwater out in the slums. Happiness is based on who you are and what you have.

MAEVE (*suddenly standing*). You know nothing –

Silence. A stand-off. CAROLYN and MAEVE refuse to see eye to eye. The others look on.

MISS BLAKE. Miss Sullivan?

MAEVE. You know nothing about it. We're scientists, aren't we? We want to be scientists. Give us a bucket of water and we will work out the laws of gravity. That costs nothing. And that is happiness. 'The mind, like its creator, is free.' John Clare.

MISS BLAKE. Well. Miss Addison?

Silence. She has no comeback.

CAROLYN. Alright.

MISS BLAKE. You know you're leagues behind the men.

Pause. MISS BLAKE takes them all in.

TESS. They've got years of schooling on us.

MISS BLAKE. But you're bright. And you're here. We're campaigning to win you the right to graduate. There's to be a vote.

CELIA. A vote?

MISS BLAKE. If Mrs Welsh can persuade the Senate, yes. They say you don't have the capacity to be scholars. So read everything. Learn everything. Know the philosophers, and then think for yourselves. For Wednesday I want three thousand words on the comparative merits of Kant's categorical imperative versus Pluralistic Deontology. And three thousand on an alternative theory.

TESS. Whose theory, ma'am?

MISS BLAKE. Your own. Now, get to a library. You know the men won't marry you if you choose knowledge. (*Pause.*) And I won't lecture you… if you don't.

Scene Four

The Wandering Womb

The young MEN *arrive in a large public lecture hall and make their way to their seats.*

LLOYD. I tell you, you could see the bones in her hand, plain as day.

EDWARDS. Her rings and the bones, but not an ounce of flesh.

HOLMES. Extraordinary.

EDWARDS. They're calling them X-rays until they think of a proper name.

HOLMES. Let me see, then.

LLOYD. Come on, Edwards.

EDWARDS. I haven't got them!

LLOYD. He has.

HOLMES. You're hiding them! He's going to claim it's his discovery!

LLOYD. Hand them over.

EDWARDS. I told you, I haven't got them!

HOLMES. Right. Search him. You take the legs.

LLOYD *and* HOLMES *go for* EDWARDS. *They might tip him upside down.*

LLOYD. They're down his trousers.

HOLMES. Get them off!

EDWARDS. Get off me, get off me! There's girls coming, look!

The WOMEN *arrive, led by their chaperone,* MISS BOTT, *who escorts them to the front row and then retreats to a seat at the side, from which she proceeds to knit loudly. The* MEN *put* EDWARDS *down.*

HOLMES. Well, well.

LLOYD. The petticoats descend.

HOLMES. So this is the future?

LLOYD. I give them about a week.

EDWARDS. I rather like them – being here – to study.

LLOYD. You can have that one at the front.

EDWARDS. You bugger off!

HOLMES. I dare you –

EDWARDS. What?

HOLMES. Speak to one.

EDWARDS. Me?

LLOYD. Go on.

EDWARDS. He'll be here any minute.

HOLMES. So crack on, old chap. Ten guineas.

LLOYD. Thirty guineas. You're in debt, Edwards. You know you need it.

EDWARDS. I can't and I won't. It's not proper.

LLOYD. Thirty guineas, Edwards. That's halfway to a stay in Paris. Imagine what would Maudie say to that.

EDWARDS. She wouldn't say anything. It's not going to happen. Alright, you're on.

EDWARDS *stands and assesses the targets.* LLOYD *helps him decide through a series of indiscreet hand signals. He picks* CELIA.

Good day.

CELIA *does not respond.*

How do you do?

She looks away.

I hope you don't mind – it's just I saw your friend over there.

He indicates MISS BOTT, *who is knitting vigorously and watching.*

She's… breathtaking. Would you mind –

MISS BOTT *stands up, suspicious, and begins advancing.*

MISS BOTT. Sir? May I help you?

EDWARDS. Damn it, she's coming over. What's her name?

MAEVE *says nothing.* TESS *is rather enjoying* HOLMES*'s joke.*

TESS (*whispered*). Miss Bott.

EDWARDS. Thank you, miss –

TESS. Moffat.

CAROLYN. Tess!

TESS. What?

EDWARDS. Oh God.

MISS BOTT. Are you causing a disturbance, sir?

EDWARDS. No, sir. Ma'am. Um, Miss – er – Bott.

LLOYD. Come on, Edwards!

EDWARDS. I just wanted to – I was so surprised – delighted – to see you – this is science – but – oh God – did you knit that yourself – oh hell.

MISS BOTT. How dare you!

EDWARDS. I'm sorry, ma'am.

He retreats.

LLOYD. Don't worry, Edwards, some women find verbal incompetence quite attractive.

The doors swing open and MR BANKS *enters.* MISS BOTT *and* EDWARDS *scuttle back to their seats, where* MISS BOTT *makes a special effort to knit extra-loudly for a couple of beats.*

MR BANKS. Gentlemen. Ladies. What a day! I haven't slept a wink! Rarely have our halls been graced by a man of such international renown. I've been trying to tempt him here for an age. Professor Maudsley's at the forefront of modern psychiatric thinking. He dines with Darwin, for Christ's sake. They're even naming a hospital after him! So please, do us proud. Be excellent.

DR MAUDSLEY has entered the room. All the students stand quickly and watch as this guru walks towards the front. MR BANKS moves to the back and watches.

Ah, Lord. Sir, you are most welcome –

DR MAUDSLEY. So, I'm told you're the best students in the world. Is that so?

EDWARDS (*standing suddenly*). Yes!

DR MAUDSLEY looks at him in surprise. EDWARDS sits down slowly.

DR MAUDSLEY. Let's not waste any time, gentlemen. We'll move straight to the crux of the matter, a subject of much current debate. The puzzling conundrum of hysteria. Hysteria meaning?

Hands raised. MISS BOTT continues to knit throughout.

You.

LLOYD. Lloyd, sir. A condition of unmanageable emotional excess.

DR MAUDSLEY. That is correct. From the Greek?

LLOYD. Hysteros, meaning uterus.

DR MAUDSLEY. Indeed. A term originally coined by Hippocrates. The hippocratic corpus was previously believed to be what, gentlemen? Yes.

HOLMES. Holmes, sir. A variety of conditions, including Heracles' disease, thought to be caused by the journey of the uterus around the body in search of vital bodily fluids.

DR MAUDSLEY. The wandering womb. Yes. Symptoms?

HOLMES. Parasthesia, muteness –

DR MAUDSLEY. And…

HOLMES. Paralysis –

DR MAUDSLEY. And…

HOLMES. Even suffocation if it reached the throat.

DR MAUDSLEY. And the remedy?

LLOYD. Pregnancy, sir. To encourage the hysteric's uterus to return to its correct location.

DR MAUDSLEY. Precisely. Now, a contemporary theory.

EDWARDS *stands*.

You.

EDWARDS. Edwards, sir. That hysteria is a sexual dysfunction which can be treated by – by stimulation. I mean, by the application of water sprays, or insertion of – vibrating – anatomical devices. (*To himself, furiously.*) What have I just said!

The MEN *smile.* DR MAUDSLEY *gives* EDWARDS *a look.*

DR MAUDSLEY. Let's abandon the fanciful speculation of the Europeans and instead turn our attention to more progressive theories. Anyone?

TESS *raises her hand. She is ignored.*

Come on, gentlemen? No one?

TESS *continues to wait with her hand raised.* LLOYD *stands.*

LLOYD. Sir.

DR MAUDSLEY. Go ahead.

LLOYD. In your thesis, you write that hysteria is brought on by a weakened morality, mind or will. That any woman is susceptible.

DR MAUDSLEY. I do indeed. And that it leads to maladies such as –

LLOYD. Mania.

DR MAUDSLEY. Yes.

HOLMES. Lunacy.

DR MAUDSLEY. Yes.

EDWARDS. Paroxysm.

DR MAUDSLEY. Yes.

LLOYD. 'Feminism.'

The MEN *might laugh.* TESS *stands.*

TESS. But, sir, I believe Charcot says hysteria is caused by specific biological weaknesses, not by a woman's lack of moral judgement at all. That it's hereditary.

A ripple of consternation.

DR MAUDSLEY. Indeed he does. Did I invite you to stand, miss?

TESS. Moffat, sir.

DR MAUDSLEY. I wasn't asking your name. I'm not interested in your name. Are you contradicting me in my own lecture?

TESS. No –

DR MAUDSLEY. Are you suggesting these Europeans are superior to my colleagues and I? Are you an expert?

TESS. No, / sir –

DR MAUDSLEY. Have you undertaken experiments? In your own laboratory?

TESS. Of course not, but, sir, these scientists –

DR MAUDSLEY. They are not scientists, they are fantasists. Miss, why are you here? This is a lecture hall, not a laundry.

TESS. Sir!

DR MAUDSLEY. Gentlemen, it has been proven time and again that hysteria results from a state of emotional agitation commonly observed in the female –

TESS. But there is no evidence to prove that / women alone are susceptible to hysteria, it's merely observation –

DR MAUDSLEY (*indicating* TESS). A woman becomes agitated as she relinquishes control of her emotions.

TESS. I am not agitated because I am a woman! / I am agitated because you won't consider an alternative scientifically proven phenomenon. What about Freud?

DR MAUDSLEY. The temperature rises, nerves destabilise, the woman begins to hyperventilate. A perfect example of hysterical agitation, gentlemen, leading to mania.

TESS. Why won't you acknowledge other people's theories?

DR MAUDSLEY. I do. Why can't you comprehend that the male organisation is one and the female quite another? You seem to think it's merely an affair of clothes.

TESS. That's not what I'm saying!

DR MAUDSLEY (*raising his voice startlingly*). Do not contradict me, miss! All you have demonstrated in your base and misguided outburst is that your sex has no capacity to control your emotional functions. (*Pause.*) Get out.

TESS. What?

DR MAUDSLEY. Out. And don't even think about coming back to a lecture of mine.

TESS *collects her belongings and leaves in silence.* MISS BOTT *tries to leave to follow her but* DR MAUDSLEY *begins again, quietly, dangerously.*

There comes a time, during a woman's pubic development, when she will expend tremendous energy in the recurring demands of menstruation. Can she bear mental drain in addition to these physical demands? The overexertion of a woman's brain, at the expense of other vital organs, may lead to atrophy, mania, or worse, may leave her incapacitated as a mother. These, sirs, are not opinions. They are facts of nature, proven by science.

(*To the* WOMEN.) I should throw the whole lot of you out.

Scene Five

Out Without Hats

The WOMEN *rush out into the street looking for* TESS. *A group of* MEN *stand chatting on the other side of the street, the* WOMEN *pay them no attention.* TESS *is distraught.*

CAROLYN. Tess!

CELIA. Are you alright?

TESS. What do you think?

CELIA. What were you doing?

TESS. I've never been spoken to like that. Never.

CELIA. Whatever will Miss Welsh say.

TESS. They can't just go on as if we weren't here.

CAROLYN. We are here. They ought to get used to it.

WILL *passes with the* MEN.

TESS. There's Will. Will!

LLOYD. Who's that then, Will?

WILL. I don't know.

TESS *approaches the* MEN.

LLOYD. Oh. Cos she seems to know you rather well.

WILL. I never…

TESS. Thank God you're here. Did you hear what happened? Why weren't you in the lecture?

WILL. I was in a tutorial.

CAROLYN. You missed quite a scene.

LLOYD. If she'd been shot out of a cannon, she'd have done less damage. (*Pause.*) So, were you planning to introduce us?

TESS. We're friends from home.

WILL. This is Miss Moffat.

LLOYD. We know exactly who she is.

Silence. WILL *looks from* TESS *to the* MEN, *confused.*

HOLMES. Can I just ask what were you thinking, miss? You
know he might well never come back. I've waited a year to
hear that man speak.

WILL. What happened?

HOLMES. Miss Moffat thought she'd set our greatest
psychiatrist straight on his amateur take on hysteria.

WILL. Blimey, Tess!

HOLMES. He advises the Royal Family! He had the floor and
he was our guest.

WILL. You spoke out?

LLOYD. Oh, come now, you didn't really expect her to know
any better, did you?

WILL. What on earth were you thinking?

TESS. Will, please!

WILL. You can't just / start –

TESS. We were told to ask questions! You could at least… I
need to go home.

She goes to leave.

LLOYD. Oh, don't go! Join us for luncheon.

HOLMES. Some other time, Lloyd.

CAROLYN. We could, couldn't we? Well, couldn't we?

LLOYD. Or dinner. Poker? You could strip Edwards of his
assets.

EDWARDS. What's left of them.

CELIA. We should go.

Meanwhile, MISS BOTT *emerges from the lecture hall.*

MISS BOTT. Ladies! No fraternising in the street! With gentlemen.

EDWARDS. It was lovely to meet you.

WILL. Tess!

MISS BOTT *herds the* WOMEN *away.*

LLOYD. Come back! (*Turning to* WILL.) Well, well, who'd have thought. Will Bennett, friend of a bluestocking.

HOLMES. And a Girtonite.

LLOYD. You didn't tell us.

WILL. You didn't ask.

HOLMES. Come on, fellas. Let's go.

LLOYD *and* HOLMES *turn to go.* WILL *follows them.*

LLOYD. Not you, Bennett. Your lot went that way.

LLOYD *exits.* EDWARDS *makes an attempt at reassuring* WILL.

HOLMES. Edwards.

EDWARDS. Sorry, Will.

LLOYD. Edwards!

EDWARDS *follows* WILL *off.* HOLMES *has a moment before exiting.*

HOLMES (*to himself*). They'll break our hearts.

Scene Six

Fragments of the World

MRS WELSH*'s office.*

TESS. I was only trying to give an educated opinion.

MRS WELSH. And was he asking for your opinion?

TESS. No, but –

MRS WELSH. Well, that's your answer.

TESS. But… (*Pause.*) I'm very sorry, ma'am.

MRS WELSH. Very sorry. Or very angry? Miss Moffat, in our first year we were in a farmhouse in Hitchin twenty miles from the city; that was considered a 'safe distance'. We had five students. We had no books, no furniture. The girls had lectures from anyone willing to risk their reputation. Yet we clung on and scrambled up and now – now we're on the brink of acceptance. Soon I'll be standing in front of the Senate asking for women's right to graduate. And if they agree to a vote, and if we win, you could be one of the first… Miss Moffat, why are you here?

TESS. To learn.

MRS WELSH. Why?

TESS. Because I want to know. About more than just myself.

MRS WELSH. And what will you do with this wealth of knowledge?

TESS. Travel the world. Chart the stars in the southern hemisphere.

MRS WELSH. So why bother getting an education? Why not just roam around Peru with a telescope.

TESS. Because I want to understand the world, not just see it.

MRS WELSH. Oh, the world? The world makes little sense to me. I've no reason to feel attached to it. I am a woman. I cannot own it. I cannot vote for who rules it. I don't even have rights over children I bring into it. Yet, very slowly, I am gaining the liberty to learn. And as I learn, I start to collect tiny pieces of knowledge, pieces which together create a little fragment of the world. And that fragment is mine. The only thing a woman can own is knowledge. And for the first time we have the opportunity to acquire it. But it's fragile. And if we allow them to think, even for a second, that we are a threat, then we set ourselves back. Patience is vital. (*With a wry smile.*) Patience and stealth. We must build our Trojan horse and infiltrate from the inside. Before they know it we will match them grade for grade. And when we do… Keep your voice soft but your brain sharp, that is the superior weapon. Do you understand?

TESS. Yes. Thank you, ma'am.

MRS WELSH. Degrees by degrees, Miss Moffat. You may go now. You have work to do.

TESS *leaves.*

We both do.

Scene Seven

The Dictionary

The WOMEN *are studying in the library, overseen by* MISS BOTT, *the chaperone. They sit together at one end of the table.* RALPH *and* LLOYD *sit reading at the other end with several other* MEN. MISS BOTT *knits loudly throughout, only stopping if something requires her attention. A weary* LIBRARIAN *sits in the corner. A long silence, everyone is working.*

RALPH *has noticed* TESS *and looks at her every so often.* TESS *notices* RALPH *and looks over. At some point, they catch each other's eye –* TESS *looks away when* RALPH *gives her a smile.*

More silence. RALPH *watches* TESS. *Another* MAN, *sitting next to him, eyes him suspiciously.* RALPH *writes a note and slips it up his sleeve. He stands and walks towards* MISS BOTT, *keeping his eyes on* TESS.

RALPH. I'm terribly sorry to bother you.

LIBRARIAN. Quiet if you please.

MISS BOTT. Yes?

RALPH (*indicating* TESS*'s book*). I believe that's the only copy. May I borrow it? I'll give it straight back.

LIBRARIAN. Quiet if you please.

RALPH (*whispers*). Sorry.

> TESS *hands the book to* MRS WELSH, *who hands it to* RALPH, *raising an eyebrow. He turns away, pretends to look something up, slips the note into the book and hands it back.*

Thanks.

LIBRARIAN. Quiet! If you please.

> *He walks towards one of the stacks.* TESS *opens the book and the note falls on the floor, seen by* MAEVE – *it's almost in* MISS BOTT*'s eye line.* MAEVE *drops her books on the floor as a distraction before* MISS BOTT *can notice the note. Then* TESS *notices it and swiftly picks it up. She gives* MAEVE *a grateful smile.*

MAEVE. Sorry, Miss Bott.

> MISS BOTT *watches them suspiciously. Silence. Everyone reads. Then she goes back to her knitting and knits loudly.*

TESS (*mouthing to* MAEVE). Thanks.

> *She looks over towards the stacks. She waits. Then she stands quietly and moves uncertainly towards the other end of the stacks.*

(*Hushed, to* MISS BOTT.) I'm just getting a –

LIBRARIAN. Quiet! Quiet.

TESS. – dictionary.

> MISS BOTT *ceases knitting for a moment. There is silence as she watches* TESS, *who pretends to look along the rows of*

books. Satisfied, MISS BOTT *goes back to her knitting.*
TESS *moves gradually closer to the stack where we can see*
RALPH *waiting through the gaps in the books. She*
disappears. We see their outlines behind the stacks and
perhaps catch a whisper or a giggle. CAROLYN *notices*
TESS *is gone. She kicks* MAEVE *under the table and*
indicates the stacks. They both lean back perilously in their
chairs trying to see. Silence while they watch and wait.
CELIA *has worked through this whole incident.*

TESS *returns from the stacks with a book.*

Found it.

She sits and continues to 'work'. CAROLYN *and* MAEVE
are trying to get her attention silently without MISS BOTT
noticing. RALPH *reappears from another stack and all eyes*
are on him as he leaves the room. He steals a look towards
TESS *as he exits.*

MAEVE (*hushed*). Be careful.

TESS. What?

CAROLYN. Who is he?

TESS *just works.* CAROLYN *tries to snatch the book which*
had the note in. TESS *gets there first.* MISS BOTT *looks up.*

TESS. I've finished, Miss Bott.

CAROLYN. I have too.

MISS BOTT. But Miss Willbond has not. You'll have to wait.

CELIA *looks up, surprised. She is gutted that they're ready*
to go so early. A moment of weighing up, then she makes a
decision – and opens a massive tome. CAROLYN *puts her*
head on the table in exasperation. LLOYD *smiles, enjoying*
the fact they're stuck. TESS *rereads the note…*

Scene Eight

The Great Escape

TESS *is in her room working. There is a knock on* TESS*'s door.*

MINNIE (*off*). Miss Moffat?

TESS. I'm working.

MINNIE (*off*). There's a young man to see you.

TESS. A young man?

MINNIE (*off*). Shall I tell them to come up?

TESS (*to herself*). Cripes! (*To* MINNIE.) Alright!

> TESS *is taken aback by this and assumes it might be*
> RALPH. *She frantically adjusts her hair and sprays cologne.*
> *Too much.*

> No. Darn it!

> *She tries to scrub it off. There is a knock.*

MISS BOTT (*off*). Moffat!

TESS. Coming! Enter!

> *The door opens to reveal* WILL *and* MISS BOTT.

> Oh. Will.

WILL. Tess. What's that smell?

TESS. Nothing.

WILL (*to* MISS BOTT). May I come in?

> MISS BOTT *nods. He enters. She follows and takes a seat.*
> *She sits silently, paying selective attention.*

> Very cosy. Who's the perfume for?

TESS. No one. I just like it.

> *This is awkward.* MISS BOTT*'s still there. They're very*
> *aware of her.*

WILL. You've made it lovely in here.

TESS. Thank you.

WILL. A woman's touch. (*Mouthing silently.*) Does she have to stay?

MISS BOTT. No male may be left unaccompanied with a female in her private quarters.

WILL. I'm hardly a threat!

MISS BOTT. No male may be left –

TESS. He's one of my oldest friends.

MISS BOTT. Rules are rules.

WILL. Of course.

> MISS BOTT *knits.* TESS *gives* WILL *a look. The following conversation is at first a little guarded, before they forget that they are being watched.*

Look. I'm sorry. About what happened in the street. It was thoughtless of me.

TESS. I don't want to talk / about it.

WILL. I didn't know what to / say.

TESS. I don't want to / talk about it.

WILL. I was with my friends. It's not easy, if you step out of line they won't let you back in.

TESS. You pretended you didn't know me, Will. I've known you most of my life.

WILL. It's different here, I can't afford to… I was worried about you. It's all very well you parading yourselves –

TESS. 'Parading'? We're not trying to make a spectacle, we're just going to lectures.

WILL. But you didn't just go to a lecture. If you were at the Newnham Girls' College you'd be thrown out. They stay in and study.

TESS. And they miss out.

WILL. They keep their reputations. If you knew what the fellas said about you, you wouldn't be seen out at all.

TESS. They can say what they like.

WILL. It's your reputation.

TESS. Don't patronise me.

WILL. Then don't be naive! I've been getting it in the neck. They barred me from the common room –

TESS. Try being a woman.

WILL. Try being responsible for a woman.

TESS. What?

WILL. I promised your father. And I won't let you down, but I'm building my career with these people. If they lose respect for me now –

TESS. This isn't about you!

WILL. Yes it is. Tess, my exams are coming up and all I can do is worry. About you.

She softens slightly.

TESS. Will.

Beat.

WILL. What's the food like here. Is it ghastly?

TESS. Will, I want this.

WILL. Is it worse than your mother's?

TESS. It's important I pass.

WILL. It's important I pass! Tess, I need to earn a living. Employers want firsts. Look, at home there are plenty of fellows who'd give their right arm for you. But three years here, they won't wait around. Your father had no idea what he was sending you into. If he'd known –

TESS. He doesn't need to know.

WILL. It's all over the papers! All this business about 'the right to graduate'. You can't hide away –

TESS. I'm not embarrassed to be here, Will, far from it.

WILL. I know that and I'm proud of you, but what happens after this? When you go home. If you lose the chance of a decent match, what'll you do?

TESS. Earn a living.

WILL. Doing what?

TESS. I want to be a scientist!

WILL. But you're a woman!

TESS. Oh, well, thank you very much, I'd almost forgotten. So what should we do, just give up?

Pause. They're both upset. He goes to hug her. They embrace.

MISS BOTT. Visitors must maintain a minimum distance of thirty inches.

WILL. I know that, thank you, Miss Bott! (*Still holding her. To* TESS.) Tess, I don't want you to regret this. The way they talk about you, I hate to hear it.

TESS. Come on, Will, don't say anything.

He won't look at her.

Have you spoken to Father? What have you said? Will!

WILL. I wrote a letter.

TESS. What?

WILL. This place.

TESS. Have you sent it?

WILL. If your reputation is damaged –

TESS. Have you sent it?

Pause.

WILL. Not yet.

TESS. You have no idea, do you?

WILL. I promised I'd look after you. Tess... (*Pause*.) When I said yes to your father, we thought you were coming here to learn. Quietly. But this! It would frighten him. It's politics. It's dangerous. No one's trying to stop you learning, but you insist on walking into a fight. It's only a certificate, you don't need one, it won't help you. Mrs Welsh doesn't have a degree and look at her. Why can't you just be content to –

TESS. Will! Just go.

WILL. What?

TESS. Just go. Please.

He stands for a moment, then leaves.

You can go now, Miss Bott.

MISS BOTT. Are you alright, miss?

TESS. No, I'm not actually.

TESS *cries.* MISS BOTT, *unsure what to do, gives* TESS *an incompetent pat on the shoulder.*

MISS BOTT. There we are then.

TESS. I'm fine. I'll be fine. Thank you.

MISS BOTT *gives her a smile and then leaves.* TESS *is left standing on her own. She then goes back to the note from* RALPH *on her desk, checks the time and makes a resolution.*

Damn this.

She puts her coat on. CAROLYN *enters.*

CAROLYN. Tess – oh! What are you doing?

TESS. What does it look like?

CAROLYN. What's that horrible smell? (*Realising*.) You're not going out, are you?!

TESS. Of course I'm not. Yes, I am.

CAROLYN. At this time of night? You can't, you'll be thrown out! Can I come?

TESS. No. How do I look?

CAROLYN. Awful. You need some powder. And some proper cologne. Wait here. (*As she exits*.) Tess?

TESS. Yes?

CAROLYN. Are you alright? I saw Will on the stairs.

TESS. Were you getting that cologne?

Beat. CAROLYN *hovers in the doorway.*

CAROLYN. I had a letter from Father today. They're staying in Paris for Christmas.

TESS (*almost ignoring her*). Oh.

Pause.

CAROLYN. What's wrong?

TESS. Nothing. Will. He just doesn't understand this. Any of it.

CAROLYN. Of course he doesn't, he's a man. You know, the Masai say 'A big goat does not stop without reason.'

TESS. Well, that's tremendous, thank you very much. I'll just grow a cassava and spear myself an antelope, shall I?

CAROLYN. Come to Paris with me.

TESS (*taken aback*). No!

CAROLYN. Say yes.

TESS. It's Christmas. I can't be away.

MAEVE *arrives in the doorway, unnoticed.*

CAROLYN. Would your folks mind?

TESS. Yes!

MAEVE. What are you doing?

CAROLYN. Maeve, you're coming to Paris.

MAEVE. What for?

CAROLYN. Because it's Christmas. And it's Paris. We'd lend you some clothes so you didn't have to wear that ghastly old grey thing.

MAEVE. I'm not coming to Paris.

CAROLYN. Tess is coming.

TESS. I'm not!

CAROLYN. So you can both buy some cologne of your own.

CAROLYN exits to get the cologne. As she goes:

Celia! Tess is going out!

CELIA (*off*). Out!

TESS (*getting ready to go*). Yes, out.

MAEVE. What are you doing?

TESS. Research.

CELIA. For what?

TESS (*with a knowing look*). Chemistry.

MAEVE. Is it that boy from the library?

CELIA arrives in the doorway, followed by CAROLYN.

CELIA. What boy from the library?

CAROLYN. Tess met a boy in the library and they were passing notes.

TESS. He's not a boy, he's a gentleman.

CELIA. Hardly, encouraging you out without a chaperone.

A knock at the door. Enter MINNIE with a coal scuttle.

MINNIE. Evening, here's your – Lord have mercy! Where are you going?

CAROLYN. Quiet, Minnie. Tess is just leaving.

TESS. How do I get down?

MINNIE. Where?

TESS. Out of the window.

CELIA. You don't.

CAROLYN. We could tie the sheets together.

TESS. What if they unravel?

MAEVE. You could die.

CELIA *turns to* MAEVE *incredulously.*

CAROLYN. You won't die if you use two sheets – you split the downward force and halve the tension.

CELIA. Only if the sum of the forces is equal to the counter-force.

TESS (*considering the danger*). Oh God.

MINNIE. I could let you out through the kitchen, miss, if you'd rather.

They all look at MINNIE. *Beat. Then all at once, relief.*

TESS. Thank you, Minnie.

MINNIE. I'll leave an apple on the window ledge.

TESS. I won't be hungry.

MINNIE. No, miss, you pick it up when you return. That way I'll know you're in and I can lock the door behind you.

CAROLYN. Have you done this before, Minnie?

MINNIE (*obviously lying*). Never, miss.

A clock strikes nine.

TESS. Alright. I'm off.

MAEVE. What's his name?

Beat. TESS *looks at them all. She's suddenly unnerved.*

TESS. I don't know.

CELIA. Where's he taking you?

TESS. I don't know.

CAROLYN. Come on, you're an adventurer. Go forth, Boadicea!

TESS. I'm hardly going to war. I met him in the library.

MINNIE. Follow me, miss. You'll have to go quietly if you're to get past Miss Bott.

CELIA. You'll regret it. She'll regret it. Tess!

TESS follows MINNIE out, the others watch. MISS BOTT sits at the end of the corridor asleep (is she?) in a rocking chair. TESS and MINNIE try to get past. Just as they are almost clear of her, MINNIE drops her keys. They freeze. MISS BOTT stirs. They sneak past. When they're gone, MISS BOTT opens her eyes.

MISS BOTT. They must think I was born yesterday.

Scene Nine

The Garden of Eden

Girton's orchard. RALPH waits leaning against a tree. TESS appears. It's dark and very quiet. She creeps to one tree. He creeps to another. She moves in the shadows from tree to tree, becoming increasingly anxious.

TESS. Curses.

He follows her. She stops under an apple tree. He creeps round the other side and puts his hand out to steady her.

RALPH. Good evening.

She screams.

It's alright, it's alright! It's alright.

TESS. Jesus!

RALPH. I'm so sorry. I didn't mean to scare you.

TESS. It's so dark, I was afraid.

RALPH. Me too. I thought your old chaperone might be on the prowl.

She giggles.

Listen, I'm sorry I asked you here. I've been paralysed with guilt.

TESS. It's alright.

An owl screeches.

RALPH. It's just a barn owl.

TESS. 'Tyto alba alba.'

RALPH. Oh, so you're a Latin scholar?

TESS. No. I'm an astrophysicist.

RALPH. Well! Me too. Venus is bright tonight.

TESS. Striking, isn't she?

RALPH. Yes, she is. (*A little moment.*) Listen, I don't even know your name.

TESS. Tess Moffat.

RALPH. Well, Miss Moffat, it's a pleasure to meet you properly.

TESS. You too.

RALPH. Ralph Mayhew. 'Esquire.'

They shake hands rather formally. Beat.

Well, this is rather unconventional, isn't it. I probably should have asked you to a clarinet concert, not to some spooky orchard.

TESS. It is a bit.

RALPH. Isn't it! (*Ghostily.*) Woooo! Look, please forgive me, I hope you don't mind; I thought I might – read you something.

TESS. Oh. Here?

RALPH. Yes. But I'm not very literary, so it might be disastrous.

TESS. I doubt that.

RALPH. It's a poem. But it's… actually, maybe I shouldn't.

TESS. No, please do.

He takes a slip of paper out, looks at it.

RALPH. I really don't know –

TESS. Go on.

RALPH. Alright. It's a love poem.

TESS. Oh.

RALPH. It's called *A Lady Who is Fair.*

TESS. Right.

RALPH.
> *Provedi, saggio, ad esta visïone,*
> *e per mercé ne trai vera sentenza.*
> *Dico: una donna di bella fazone,*
> *di cu' el meo cor gradir molto s'agenza.*
> *mi fe' d'una ghirlanda donagione,*
> *verde, fronzuta, con bella accoglienza.*

Pause.

TESS. Well that was –

RALPH. That's not the end.

TESS. Oh. Right.

RALPH.
> *Appresso mi trovai per vestigione*
> *camicia di suo dosso, a mia parvenza.*
> *Allor di tanto, amico, mi francaiche*
> *dolcemente presila abbracciare.*

Pause.

That's the end.

TESS. Well! Well. That was quite beautiful. Thank you. What does it mean?

RALPH (*doesn't know Italian*). Well, it's about a lady... who is fair... and she, well, she... it's very... (*Pause.*) You know, Italian's not really my forte. I'm a scientist. Maybe next time I'll show you an experiment.

TESS. I should like that.

RALPH. Or I could write you a paper on Kepler.

TESS. How do you know I like Kepler?

RALPH. Your book, in the library.

TESS. So you knew I was an astronomer!

RALPH. I was impressed.

TESS. You don't think it's unfeminine?

RALPH. Anyone who can make head or tail of Kepler deserves a medal in my book. I'm using my copy as a doorstop. I think you being here – ladies studying – well, it's grand.

TESS. We don't hear that very often.

He looks at her fondly, then takes a risk.

RALPH. Miss Moffat, may I kiss your hand?

TESS *extends her hand. He takes it and kisses it politely. He holds on to it for just a second.*

You're getting cold. You mustn't stay out any longer.

TESS. Thank you for your unusual poem. May I keep it?

RALPH. They say it's the most beautiful love poem ever written.

TESS. I wonder what Shakespeare would say to that?

RALPH. He'd probably pinch it. Maybe you should keep it under your hat.

TESS. I'll do just that.

She loosens her hat and takes it off. He places the poem on her head carefully, holding it there for a second as she puts her hat back on. They look at each other for a moment.

RALPH. So, goodnight, Miss Moffat.

TESS. Goodnight.

She walks back towards the door. He begins to walk away.

Wait! How will I know…?

RALPH. I'll leave you a sign. Look out for it. Goodnight, sweet mistress!

TESS. Goodnight.

She watches him until he is out of sight. Then she has a little moment of elation before she exits.

Scene Ten

The Merits of Moral Science

The WOMEN *are in their moral science class with* MISS BLAKE, *who is full of gusto.*

MISS BLAKE. So, you were barred from another lecture, I hear.

CAROLYN. We were turned away at the door.

MISS BLAKE. Again? Well, this is becoming quite a page-turner. You know, it makes me wonder if there's any point teaching you at all. Especially moral science. You're dismissed. (*Packs to go.*)

CAROLYN. What?

MISS BLAKE. Free to go.

TESS. Miss Blake!

CELIA. You can't just leave us!

MISS BLAKE. Why not? The world hurtles forward. What's the point of the arts when technology evidently needs you. Go on. I'm wasting your time. Moral science? Pah! And classics, literature, music – worthless. Nothing compared to science and mathematics. We philosophers and poets have nothing to offer you.

CAROLYN. That's not true, ma'am.

MISS BLAKE. Why not?

CAROLYN. We learn science through the arts, don't we? We study reason and logic when we read Galileo and Copernicus.

MISS BLAKE. You're still arguing that science is the highest form of knowledge.

TESS. But what if it is, ma'am?

MISS BLAKE. Go on.

TESS. Well, science improves our lives in practical ways which the arts cannot.

MISS BLAKE. Well put. Now if that's really your opinion, get out.

TESS. Why?

MISS BLAKE. Unless you can argue my position.

TESS. But what if I don't agree with it?

MISS BLAKE. A fine theorist can argue either side of the debate. Why might the arts be superior to natural science? Give me a contemporary thinker.

CAROLYN. Arnold, ma'am.

MISS BLAKE. Good God, Miss Addison, you've discovered the library!

CAROLYN. Arnold said that science doesn't address the bigger questions. What it means to be human. What intellect is, what beauty is.

TESS. We can't advance as a nation if we live out of history books.

CAROLYN. But literature elevates us beyond science. Science is elementary. What a body is, how it functions. It doesn't address why it exists. Arts asks us more. What does it mean to be? What is truth? What is love?

CELIA. Science is all about seeking truth, but in reality, not in fanciful ideas.

CAROLYN. Love isn't fanciful. It can be felt, experienced.

Voices begin to be raised a little.

CELIA. But it's not real. It's not tangible.

TESS. Lovers are tangible.

MISS BLAKE (*warning her jovially*). Miss Moffat.

TESS. Come on. If your lover had the pox, you'd rather a doctor treat him than an artist drown him with poetry.

CAROLYN. How do you know what my lover wants?

CELIA. Tess is right. Science can save lives.

TESS. And arts can't.

CAROLYN. But if your lover was dying, and there was nothing in the world but machinery – if there was nothing to elate him, if the world was barren of poetry and music, then there'd be little reason to revive him. It's the arts that make his life worth sustaining.

MISS BLAKE. Well said, Miss Addison.

CAROLYN. Well, I don't believe it entirely. I'm still going to be a doctor.

MAEVE (*in a sudden outburst*). We're all missing the point.

Pause.

MISS BLAKE (*surprised*). Miss Sullivan?

MAEVE. All the great scientists, Copernicus, Galileo, they made their discoveries because they had imagination. They saw more than what was in front of them; they thought like artists! They dreamed. And painters, great painters, treat their art like a science. Van Gogh did countless experiments with tone to work out the effects of darkness and light. They're renaissance men. Proper thinkers. That's what progress needs. The fellows out there, building the chapel – they measure the timber so the vaults can bear weight – but without the stories in the stained glass – well, then it would be no more than a barn.

MISS BLAKE. And who said that?

MAEVE. Ma'am?

MISS BLAKE. Which philosopher?

MAEVE (*cautiously*). No philosopher. It's just what I think.

MISS BLAKE. And that is why I shall not be cancelling my classes. The value of your lessons isn't knowledge. It is the fact that you are learning to think. You're making progress, ladies! I'll tell you what. Leave your books. I defy any of you to doubt in the merits of the arts when you've had a good look at the revolutionary work of Mr van Gogh.

There is a moment of communion between the WOMEN, *then they follow* MISS BLAKE *out, elated.*

Scene Eleven

An Arrival

In the foyer. MINNIE *is dusting,* CAROLYN *is passing through.*

CAROLYN. Minnie. I've left some purchases in the hall. Can you deal with them?

MINNIE. Yes, miss. What are they?

CAROLYN. Afghan hounds. Two of them. They're absolutely stunning, but they don't do what they're told.

MINNIE. Miss, it's supposed to be no pets.

CAROLYN. That's why you have to hide them.

MINNIE. Where? Under the bed!

CAROLYN. Oh no, they're enormous. Now what have you done with Achilles?

MINNIE. I sold him.

CAROLYN is lost for words, before she realises MINNIE *is joking.*

BILLY. Excuse me.

They turn around to see BILLY *in the doorway. He's rough-looking, poorly dressed.*

I'm here to see my sister.

MINNIE. Sir, if you could just wait there. (*Running off.*) Mrs Welsh, there's a man in the building!

TESS *enters.*

TESS. A man in the building?

CAROLYN. Yes, a man in the building.

BILLY. I'm here to see my sister.

TESS. Who are you?

CELIA *appears.*

CELIA. What's going on? (*Seeing* BILLY.) Oh Lord. There's a man in the building!

MRS WELSH *appears.*

MRS WELSH. A man in the building? Ladies, make yourselves decent. May I help you?

BILLY. I need to speak to Maeve.

MRS WELSH. Ah, Mr Sullivan.

BILLY. Look, lady, just tell me where my sister is.

MRS WELSH. If you could be patient / for a moment.

BILLY. I need to see her now. Maeve!

MRS WELSH. Mr Sullivan, you are welcome at Girton but whilst you are here you must respect our rules so please don't threaten us.

MAEVE *appears.*

MAEVE. Billy? What are you doing here? (*Pause.*) Billy?

BILLY. Maeve. You look different.

MAEVE. Thanks. You too.

UNIVERSITY OF WINCHESTER
LIBRARY

BILLY. Not surprising. It's been a long time.

MAEVE. How are you?

BILLY. Ah, you know.

MRS WELSH. Mr Sullivan –

BILLY. Look. We can talk later. You gotta come with me.

MAEVE. What are you talking about?

BILLY. You're coming with me. I'm taking you home.

MAEVE. I'm not going anywhere.

BILLY. You are.

MAEVE. You've got no right / to walk in here like this.

BILLY. I've got every right. Don't make me drag you out of here.

MRS WELSH. That's enough! This is a ladies' college.

BILLY. She's not a lady.

MRS WELSH. She's a member of this college and while she's under my roof –

BILLY. You got to come home.

MAEVE. I'm not coming home, Billy.

BILLY. We need you.

MAEVE. You can manage. You said.

BILLY. Things are different now.

MAEVE. Don't, Billy.

   MISS BLAKE *enters*.

MISS BLAKE. What's going on?

TESS. It's her right to be here.

BILLY. Here? This isn't her world. (*To* MAEVE.) You're not one of them. Look at you.

MAEVE. I took the examinations. I work hard. / I've got good marks. If you'd just listen to me for one – just for one minute, Billy!

BILLY. Examinations? They don't make no difference. Not out there – there, where you left the rest of us.

MRS WELSH. Mr Sullivan, your mother and I made an agreement. Lady Beaumont provides you with an allowance so that Maeve can study. It has worked perfectly well so far. She's an extraordinary student.

BILLY. No good though, is it, being extraordinary at books when there's a babe and young 'uns with no one to mother them.

MAEVE. What?

BILLY. You heard.

MAEVE. What's happened to Mother?

BILLY. Oh, now the concern –

MAEVE. Billy, where's Mother?

BILLY. She's dead, Maeve.

Beat.

MAEVE. What? Dead?

BILLY. She… there was… I can't say, Maeve. Not here.

MAEVE. She's dead? Dead?

BILLY. I tried to send word but couldn't find anyone to write me a letter. Just my coming here's lost me my job. With the big ships they don't hang about, and the yards have their own law, the police daren't set foot in them. I can't mess them about. I can't work and look after the girls. You got to come home.

Beat.

MAEVE. Did she suffer? Ma?

BILLY *can't answer. Beat.*

I can't.

BILLY. What? What do you mean 'you can't'?

MAEVE. I can't come home.

BILLY. What?

MAEVE. This is my home.

BILLY. But what about us?

TESS. This is her home.

BILLY. What would you know?

MRS WELSH. We understand –

BILLY. How could you understand? We don't have nothing.
The girls won't survive, miss!

MAEVE. I can't do it, Billy.

BILLY. You have to. Maeve? Maeve! (*To* MRS WELSH.) Tell
her. Tell her she has to come home. They're her sisters. Your
sisters, Maeve. We won't survive!

MRS WELSH. Maeve, listen / to me.

MAEVE. I can't. I can't go back.

BILLY. You have to! Tell her she has to, miss. You can't just…
(*Beat.*) Is that it? You're just going to… (*Beat.*) You're like
he was.

MAEVE. I'm nothing like he was.

BILLY. You're just like him. Dear God, Maeve. I can't even
look at you.

He leaves. There is a long pause.

MAEVE. I am sorry, ma'am. I didn't know…

MRS WELSH. You weren't to know.

MAEVE. Thank you for sending him away.

MRS WELSH. Miss Sullivan. I'm afraid you'll need to pack
your bags.

MAEVE. Ma'am?!

MRS WELSH. You must go to your room and pack.

TESS. You can't.

CELIA. You can't do that!

MISS BLAKE. Mrs Welsh! Please don't be rash.

MRS WELSH. You have brothers and sisters you are responsible for.

MAEVE. I didn't bear them. I didn't choose them.

MRS WELSH. They need a mother.

MAEVE. But this is who I am! You gave me this chance, you've shown me the world! I never knew what I wanted before, before I came here, and now I've found it, I've seen what the world is, I'm learning, I've learnt who I am. Don't take that away, please!

MISS BLAKE. Mrs Welsh –

MAEVE. I'd rather kill myself. I'll throw myself under the train.

MRS WELSH. Please don't make this any more difficult than it needs to be.

MAEVE. It's cos of where I'm from, isn't it? Cos I'm not like them. Cos I needed help.

MRS WELSH. You know perfectly well that's not true.

MAEVE. You only want respectable girls from respectable families. Not slummers' drudge like me.

MRS WELSH. Don't you dare suggest that.

MAEVE. But it's my life, Mrs Welsh! I'm going to be a teacher. And I understand people – I've lived. (*Silence*.) Please, this is my only chance.

MISS BLAKE. Mrs Welsh, can't we at least talk about this?

Silence. MRS WELSH *looks round at them all.*

MRS WELSH. Ladies, don't you have work to do? Miss Sullivan, I'm afraid you'll be leaving us in the morning.

The WOMEN *all exit, including* MAEVE. TESS *is hugely upset and walks into her room, where we see her begin to write. This continues under the next scene.*

MISS BLAKE. What are you doing?

MRS WELSH. I'm sorry?

MISS BLAKE. She's the brightest student here.

MRS WELSH. And the lives of young children are at stake!

MISS BLAKE. They'd manage. They have a community.

MRS WELSH. Imagine what the papers would say – a girl's learning more important than children's lives?

MISS BLAKE. It's not about profile!

MRS WELSH. Everything we do is about profile. We're a public establishment. You remember what it was like when you were a student in Hitchin.

MISS BLAKE. Yes, I do. You showed us that we have a choice.

MRS WELSH. Money gives you choice. Maeve doesn't have that.

MISS BLAKE. So we'll pack her off to be a mother, will we? What sort of signal does that send out? It goes against everything we're fighting for.

MRS WELSH. *We* are not fighting, Miss Blake. We are not suffragists. I'll thank you to keep them well and truly out of the building.

MISS BLAKE. They're strong allies.

MRS WELSH. They're radicals. And the girls' right to graduate hangs in the balance!

MISS BLAKE. Maeve has no rights, and we don't even have the vote. If we'd had that when they were voting on the Crimea, you might not be a widow now.

Silence.

MRS WELSH. I want the vote too. So much. But we cannot compromise. Any association with those women will finish us. This is a great loss. And not just for Maeve, for us too. I wish there was another way, but I have no choice.

They part.

There's to be no more talk of suffrage. Not in class. Not at all.

Scene Twelve

Science of the Heart

MR BANKS *is handing back the* MEN*'s essays.*

MR BANKS. Lloyd, a virtuoso display of facts, just check your light energies. Bennett, good detail… very good. Edwards, I learnt a great deal about metamorphic rock. It's astonishing work. There's strawberry jam on your conclusion.

EDWARDS. I went to Lyme Regis for research, sir.

HOLMES. It wasn't all science, sir. He took Maudie with him.

LLOYD. For the ride.

EDWARDS. We're inseparable.

RALPH. He asked her to marry him. And she said yes.

MR BANKS. Good man, Edwards.

LLOYD. She's quite something, sir.

EDWARDS. She's a taller lady, sir, but she's glorious.

Pause.

MR BANKS (*referencing their essays*). These 'wonders of the human mind'. They're articulate, they're accurate. They're first class. But there's something missing.

HOLMES. Sir?

MR BANKS. Spirit. Panache.

WILL. Oh, come on, sir.

RALPH. I'd love to be a poet, sir, but we're scientists, aren't we.

MR BANKS. Agreed. But I'll give you a shilling if you can name a scientist who wasn't passionate about his discoveries. We must be hunters, explorers. Holmes, what excites you?

HOLMES. That'd be telling, sir.

MR BANKS. Come on.

HOLMES. I'm a violinist.

LLOYD. And a Blue on the track.

HOLMES. I play with the chamber orchestra.

MR BANKS. Alright. So endless hours of practice, broken fingernails, neighbours in a fury – why do you do it?

HOLMES. Well, on the track, it's practice. Speed. Precision. But in the orchestra… it's beyond that somehow. The tone we aim for is nothing to do with practice. It's more than the sum of the sounds. It's like an opiate. Beethoven said music was beyond any wisdom or philosophy. It's like trying to get to something – more.

MR BANKS. 'Something more.' Exactly. Lloyd?

LLOYD. I went up the Matterhorn, sir, with an international team.

MR BANKS. Go on, tell us more.

LLOYD. They asked us to the Palace when we got back.

MR BANKS. You haven't answered my question.

LLOYD. Alright. Well, we tried for the Furggen Ridge but there was an avalanche, so we went up the south face instead. It's fourteen thousand feet of sheer cliff face, sir. Rocks and glacial ice. Seventy-two-hours-straight climb, and we did it without ropes. Before the summit the fog was so thick that I had to feel my way on my hands and knees. But when we got through the clouds, it's just you and the sky. It made me believe in God. We lost a man, sir. But I'd do it again, no question.

MR BANKS. Thank you, Lloyd. Edwards?

HOLMES. Maudie. She's his conquest, sir.

RALPH. She's his life.

MR BANKS. Alright then. Edwards is off gallivanting with his intended along the seafront. He admires the cliffs.

EDWARDS. Cretaceous chalk, sir.

MR BANKS. The sunlight in her hair. He allows his arm to brush up against hers.

EDWARDS. Steady on, sir.

MR BANKS. It's thrilling. It's new. He feels something bubbling deep down.

EDWARDS. Dutch courage, sir.

MR BANKS. No. It's passion.

EDWARDS. Sir!

MR BANKS. Exhilaration. And yet what have I got here? An essay that's as dry as old soot. When what I need is the lust for discovery you feel about Maudie, in your essay. How does it feel?

EDWARDS. Don't ask me that, sir! Ask Mayhew. He's got a girl.

MR BANKS. So… what's it like?

Silence.

Mayhew?

RALPH. Oh, come on.

MR BANKS. Mayhew?

Silence.

RALPH. Alright. It feels – important. Necessary.

HOLMES. Oy oy!

RALPH. Come on, I'm not talking about *that*. I'm just saying – I'm interested – in everything.

LLOYD. And therefore is winged cupid painted blind.

RALPH. All I'm saying is, when she talks I just – want to know. I can't explain it. She's vital.

Pause.

MR BANKS. Bennett, you're quiet today. What makes you happy?

WILL. Sir. This does, sir. This does, absolutely.

TESS *finishes her essay and folds it, as* MR BANKS *unfolds the first copy of the essay.*

MR BANKS. You are excellent students, gentlemen, but to change the world you must harness that urge to question. Be hungry. Dig deeper. (*Hands* LLOYD *the essay.*) And it might even be a double first, Lloyd.

LLOYD. Oh, I don't think so, sir.

MR BANKS *hands copies out to everyone.*

MR BANKS. I want you to read this for tomorrow. Read and take note.

WILL. This isn't a second-year essay, surely.

MR BANKS. Oh, it is, Bennett. But there's something more there, isn't there.

RALPH (*reading*). This is more than science.

MR BANKS. It means something to the writer. Go on now. Get out of here.

The MEN *don't move; they are all reading the essay.*

EDWARDS. Sir?

MR BANKS. Edwards?

EDWARDS. Whose essay is this?

LLOYD. Do we know him?

MR BANKS. I don't think so.

HOLMES. Was he a Trinity fellow?

MR BANKS. Trinity? No, no. Girton.

EDWARDS. He was – *she* was –

MR BANKS. Good day, boys.

MR BANKS *leaves. The* MEN *stand in silence.*

Scene Thirteen

An Education

MRS WELSH *stands and addresses the gathered Senate members. She has a leaflet in her hand.*

MRS WELSH. Gentlemen, the graduation of women. I'm going to surprise you by being brief. I only have one suggestion to put to you; that a student's mind might be bright enough to transcend their gender.

I have here an essay given to me by Professor Banks. In it the student combines physics with study of Kepler and the ancient texts to explain the existence of the Star of Bethlehem. For many years, St Matthew's narrative has puzzled scientists. He describes a star brighter than anything else in the sky, which rises in the east, moves towards Jerusalem, and then changes course to travel south as it guides the Magi towards Bethlehem. If I may quote you just a few lines:

'There is no physical possibility of a star changing course. So what did the Wise Men see? Consider the possibility of an optical illusion. Just as a cart on the road ahead appears to move backwards when overtaken, when the Earth passes Jupiter that October at a rate of twelve to one, onlookers at a specific longitude would have witnessed the planet seeming to double back on itself in retrograde motion. To the Magi standing at thirty-four degrees east in Jerusalem, Jupiter would have appeared to shift from its easterly course onto a new trajectory, north-west, towards Bethlehem.

As for the mystery of its brightness, that October, Saturn and Jupiter aligned in Pisces, a once-in-a-millennia occurrence, the resplendent glow twice as bright as anything else in the heavens. And this had great theological significance. Jupiter is the Roman symbol of kings, Saturn, the symbol of Israel, and Pisces, the symbol of the Jews. There it was, above them, "Here is the King of Israel, King of the Jews", written in the stars.'

Meanwhile, CELIA, CAROLYN *and* TESS *gather at the top of the stairs.*

CAROLYN. She hasn't gone, has she?

TESS. We'd have seen her.

CELIA. Poor Maeve.

MAEVE*'s door opens and she comes out holding her coat, followed by* MINNIE *who carries her suitcase. She walks past each of the* WOMEN, *each of whom smiles at her.* MRS WELSH *continues.*

MRS WELSH. A remarkable mind in the making. And yet, this morning I let another equally gifted student go, as family circumstances demanded it. We will not allow scholarship to sabotage home life, gentlemen. But, where it can be taken up without compromise, the benefits will radiate from that student to everyone who surrounds them. So giving our girls an education won't only mean better nurses and teachers. It'll brighten the world for our sons and daughters for generations to come.

Gentlemen, I ask you please to consider a full membership vote.

MAEVE *reaches the door, then turns back.*

MAEVE. I hope you win. The vote.

CELIA. Thank you, Maeve.

MAEVE. Thank you.

MRS WELSH. Thank you.

Curtain.

ACT TWO

Scene One

An Offer

In a staffroom at Trinity College. MR BANKS *has just entered.*
RADLEIGH, ANDERSON *and* COLLINS *are standing around
a table.*

MR BANKS. I wasn't expecting a reception committee.

ANDERSON. Well, congratulations are in order. We hear Lloyd
and Bennett are on track for firsts next year.

MR BANKS. Yes.

ANDERSON. You'll be next in line for a sainthood, flashing
miracles like that.

MR BANKS. They've turned themselves round.

COLLINS. You've turned them around, Banks.

MR BANKS. I love my work.

ANDERSON. Your results speak for themselves. It's secured
our place at the top of the league. Which is rather fortunate
timing. You see, we're looking to offer a new fellowship.

MR BANKS. A fellowship?

ANDERSON. Yes, indeed.

MR BANKS. That's excellent news for Trinity.

A pause.

ANDERSON. Well?

MR BANKS. Well what?

ANDERSON. Really, Banks, for a double-first scholar you're a
bit slow on the uptake.

MR BANKS. You mean me?

ANDERSON. Yes, you!

MR BANKS. Well, I – I never expected – / thank you, thank you so much.

COLLINS. Well deserved, Banks.

RADLEIGH. Banks.

MR BANKS. Bloody hell! What will my wife say!

RADLEIGH. It's quite an honour. She ought to be grateful.

MR BANKS. Thank you, thanks! Thank you all.

ANDERSON. We should have a toast.

He rings a bell.

Of course, it will mean attendance at various functions, drinks, dinners –

MR BANKS. How will I cope!

ANDERSON. There'll be superior accommodation, security and tenure. You might get a view of the garden.

MR BANKS. What can I say? I'm delighted!

COLLINS. We can see that!

MR BANKS. When would it start?

ANDERSON. September, but the rooms can be freed up this term.

MR BANKS. I'll need to reorganise my timetables –

ANDERSON. You might like to think about dropping your external commitments.

MR BANKS. It's not many hours, I assure you. Mrs Welsh is aware of my duties here.

COLLINS. Of course, but this is a full-time post.

MR BANKS. I understand, but –

RADLEIGH. You simply won't have time.

MR BANKS. But I made a commitment there. They're very talented students.

COLLINS. And it's your level of commitment that makes you ideal, as a fellow.

MR BANKS. Yes, good. Thank you.

Pause.

ANDERSON (*carefully*). I think perhaps you misunderstand. It won't be possible for you to continue teaching at Girton once you are a fellow of Trinity.

RADLEIGH. It is unsuitable.

MR BANKS. But surely there is a way to –

COLLINS. There is no way. A fellow can't be seen to fritter away his time in the pursuit of ladies' 'education'.

MR BANKS. 'Fritter away'?

COLLINS. That's what I said.

RADLEIGH. What did I tell you?

ANDERSON (*taking him slightly to one side*). Difficult this, Thomas.

MR BANKS. It's unthinkable.

ANDERSON. Please be sensible.

COLLINS. You were rather a controversial choice, Banks.

RADLEIGH. Controversial? Bloody madness.

COLLINS. You wouldn't embarrass Mr Anderson, would you? He put a lot on the line offering you this post. We weren't all convinced.

MR BANKS. Gentlemen. I need time to think.

ANDERSON. What's there to think about? It's security for life, Banks.

MR BANKS. I understand, but they're halfway through their course.

COLLINS. You won't lose out by leaving Girton.

MR BANKS. I'm sorry, that's simply not true.

COLLINS. It's just a hobby for them. They're not undergraduates.

MR BANKS. They may be soon, if the vote goes our way –

RADLEIGH. *Our* way?

Beat. He realises he's overstepped the mark.

MR BANKS (*reluctantly*). If the vote… if the vote goes in favour of the women. Graduating.

Beat. The TRINITY MEN *share a look*. MR BANKS *has blown it.*

Please, gentlemen. I just need to think. I need some time.

RADLEIGH. Have you thought about what they might want? In the future? They just don't know it yet. My wife has a life she wouldn't give up. We dine with twenty families. She runs the Lolworth Fair. She takes the Coram orphans to the Whitsun Parade. These girls will never be wives. They'll sacrifice all of that. And for what? They might want to be scientists, they won't be. So where does that leave them? I wouldn't want it for my daughter, Banks, not a chance. It's irresponsible.

RADLEIGH *storms out*. MR BANKS *is reeling*. COLLINS *follows* RADLEIGH *out.*

COLLINS. Mr Banks. Thank you for your time.

MR BANKS (*to* ANDERSON). Jonathan… please…

ANDERSON *stands and follows the other two out*. MR BANKS *is left there alone. A* MAID *arrives with a tray containing a bottle of champagne and four glasses.*

Scene Two

The Telescope

TESS, CAROLYN *and* CELIA *are doing the cancan in the drawing room.* CAROLYN *shouts instructions,* CELIA *dances with surprising abandon. All three have their skirts hitched up around their middles.*

CAROLYN. Blimey, Celia!

Then the door opens and MISS BLAKE *enters with* MISS BOTT *and* WILL, *who is holding a wrapped gift.* CELIA *sees* WILL *and suddenly panics. She trips.*

CELIA (*falling*). Oh God!

The WOMEN *fall down like dominoes.*

MISS BLAKE. No no, do carry on.

CAROLYN. We saw the cancan in Paris.

TESS. And we were teaching Celia.

CAROLYN. Though she's completely out of control.

CELIA. Carolyn!

MISS BLAKE. That's not like you, Celia.

CELIA. Argh, I think I've twisted it.

MISS BOTT. Out of the way. Leave it to me.

CELIA *and* TESS *help* CELIA *to a chair.* MISS BLAKE *goes to help* CELIA *but* MISS BOTT *swoops in and takes over.*

CAROLYN. Mrs Welsh said we could perform it at the end of term.

MISS BLAKE. Has she seen it?

CELIA (*to* CAROLYN). You asked if we could perform a French folk dance. You never said it was the cancan!

MISS BLAKE. So, did she tell you the news?

CAROLYN. What news?

TESS. Is there news?

MISS BLAKE. We heard yesterday.

CAROLYN. What…

TESS. The vote…

MISS BLAKE. Yes!

TESS. We didn't get it?!

MISS BLAKE. We did! We got it!

Jubilation.

It's hard to believe but we did! You should have heard her speak.

CAROLYN. What did she say?

MISS BLAKE. Never mind that. The Senate didn't know what to do with themselves. They agreed that your right to graduate is at least a vote-worthy issue, though only university members can vote.

CELIA. So none of us? What?

MISS BLAKE. No women at all. And no undergraduates. So write to everyone you know. Times are changing, ladies.

TESS. Imagine. Maybe one day we'll have even have a voice.

MISS BLAKE. And, the most remarkable woman is coming to Cambridge to speak. Millicent Fawcett.

CAROLYN. The suffragist? The one in the papers.

MISS BLAKE. Yes. There's to be a rally on Saturday. It'll be quite the occasion.

TESS. We can organise support –

MISS BLAKE. I think it's best not to publicise it too much. I wouldn't trouble Mrs Welsh with it.

TESS. But she's the one who put all the work in.

MISS BLAKE. Suffrage is political. We have to be careful.

TESS. We understand.

MISS BLAKE. Thank you. Now, I'll leave you to it, Miss Bott.

She leaves.

CAROLYN. Oh, Miss Bott, we brought you a present from Paris.

MISS BOTT. For me? Well. Most kind.

CAROLYN *hands her a box, which she opens.*

What's this? Crustaceans?

CAROLYN. Escargot. They're Parisian.

MISS BOTT. That's hardly a recommendation. Be gone with you! I'm sure Mr Bennett has no interest in being entertained by the whole pack of you.

CELIA *tries to walk but can't.*

TESS. Are you alright?

CELIA. No.

MISS BOTT. I told you, nothing good comes out of France. You'll have to come with me to get that seen to.

CAROLYN. I'll help.

MISS BOTT. No male may be left alone with a female.

CAROLYN. Oh, Miss Bott! I'll stay here. Will, don't even touch her.

WILL *puts his hands up, protesting his innocence.* MISS BOTT *helps* CELIA *out.*

MISS BLAKE. Miss Addison, I hope I can trust you.

CAROLYN. With your life, Miss Bott.

CELIA *hobbles out, leaning on* MISS BOTT. *As she exits…*

MISS BOTT. I thought you understood the laws of gravity. (*Without looking back.*) Miss Addison, don't even think about it.

As soon as MISS BOTT *is out of sight –*

CAROLYN. I'll be off then.

TESS. Thanks, Caro.

She goes, leaving WILL *and* TESS *alone.* WILL *is agitated.*

WILL. Hello. Happy New Year.

TESS. Happy New Year.

WILL. So…

TESS. So…

WILL. Christmas was quiet. (*Indicates her hitched-up skirts.*) Is this the French fashion?

She pulls her skirts down.

TESS. You don't have to come here. We're hardly respectable company.

He hands her a gift.

WILL. Merry Christmas. Happy New Year. It's a telescope.

TESS (*taken aback*). Oh.

WILL. Well, open it then.

TESS. Did you wrap it yourself?

WILL. No. The lady in the shop did it.

TESS. Will, you shouldn't have. (*Unwraps the telescope.*) Oh! You can't afford this!

WILL. Well, Banks thinks you're going somewhere in astronomy, so –

He steps out through the French windows.

TESS. How do you know? Where are you going?

WILL. To get some air. You're lucky, having an orchard here. I read your essay, about the Star. We all did. But your maths is out. Jupiter's elliptical orbit is inclined, even on the Cavendish equipment. It can throw you out by a mile, or well, forty-six-million miles, and Tess, I think I might have fallen in love with you.

TESS. Oh. I see.

WILL. Well. I'll try and fall out again.

TESS. Will –

WILL. It's hardly convenient, is it.

TESS (*surprised, kindly*). No.

WILL. What did you do for Christmas lunch?

TESS. Lunch? We went out. Some fancy restaurant.

WILL. You went out?

TESS. It was different.

WILL. My mother burnt the turkey.

TESS. She always burns the turkey. Will – last term, one afternoon in the library… there was a scientist. He wrote me a note. A poem. And…

WILL. Oh. I see. And it's… he's… you two are…

TESS. It looks that way.

WILL. I didn't know. Well. There we are then. (*Pause.*) Your father missed you.

TESS. How is he?

WILL. Fine.

TESS. You didn't say anything about the trouble we're in or the graduation vote?

WILL. I told him you were working hard.

TESS. Thank you.

WILL. He ate too much. And Miss Pope came round.

TESS. Miss Pope!

WILL. She ate too much.

TESS. Will…

WILL. I know, but she's due to inherit and she's my age, so there's a match.

TESS. But she's…

WILL. I know. But. Has this scientist told you his intentions?

TESS. He cares for me a great deal.

WILL. And do you trust him?

TESS. Yes, I think so.

WILL. What's his name? Actually, don't tell me, I don't want to know. Your father will want to meet him.

TESS. Yes, if it comes to that. I'm sorry. Are you alright? (*Pause.*) Will you visit again soon?

WILL. I have to study. End of year, you know how it is. But if you need me, you know where I am.

MISS WELSH *enters*.

MRS WELSH. Tess Moffat. I hear you're responsible for Miss Willbond's accident.

TESS. I was only –

MRS WELSH. What were you thinking?

TESS. Ma'am.

MRS WELSH. The cancan!

TESS. It's a French folk dance.

MRS WELSH. I know full well what sort of folk dance like that. You will forfeit your excursion rights for the weekend.

TESS. Ma'am.

MRS WELSH. Sir, you know the rules.

WILL. Don't worry, ma'am. There's no danger of anything untoward. We're just old friends. Will you excuse me.

WILL *goes to leave*.

TESS (*after him*). No, Will!

MRS WELSH. Calculus. Now.

TESS. Yes, ma'am.

Scene Three

Time Travellers

Later the same evening, TESS *and* RALPH *arrive on a hilltop.*

TESS. It's like being on top of the world.

RALPH. Look, there's King's. And Girton!

TESS. And Orion. Up there.

RALPH. You didn't even look.

TESS. I don't need to. I know where it is.

RALPH. Alright, what else is up there? Don't look up!

They continue talking but looking at each other, not at the sky.

TESS. Aries in the west.

RALPH. Perseus.

TESS. Pleiades, the seven sisters –

RALPH. You know they say Orion fell so desperately in love with them that he chased them right across the world. So Zeus turned them into stars, to keep them safe. All but the youngest. Merope. She'd fallen in love with a human.

TESS. What happened to her?

RALPH. I think they stole away, the two of them. He took her somewhere where no one could find them. That's why they thought there were only six stars in Pleiades.

TESS. Until they invented telescopes.

RALPH. Tess, it's good to see you. You are brave.

TESS. I'm an outlaw! (*Pause.*) Why would he want to hide her away?

RALPH. Because he wanted to keep her safe. (*Pause.*) I went to the observatory this afternoon. I looked for the seventh star, but I couldn't see her. There was a smudge on the lens. And my mind was elsewhere.

TESS. Why?

RALPH. Just… because.

A moment.

TESS. That wasn't a smudge – it's Andromeda.

RALPH. It was a smudge. Are you sure?

TESS. If you're looking at the 'W' of Cassiopeia, the two end stars point directly at it. It just looks like a smudge because it's so distant. It's so odd – what we see now, that's how it was two million years ago. That light started its journey to us before humans had even arrived on the earth.

RALPH. We're like time travellers. I wonder what it looks like now?

TESS. We'll never know.

RALPH. Maybe there'll be another pair of stargazers, in two million years, staring at Andromeda, wondering the same thing.

TESS. In two million years! I wonder what else they'll be thinking.

RALPH. That he wouldn't swap this for anything in the world. There's no one like you, Tess Moffat.

They might kiss…

Scene Four

Bread and Circuses

MR PECK *is pulling the cart along. Inside it,* CAROLYN *is hiding under the blanket.*

MR PECK. No one but me would be this daft… this is a bad idea. A bad idea! She'll find us out, I tell you. 'Mr Peck, what are you doing?' 'Nothing, ma'am.' 'Why are you taking the cart out?' 'I'm not taking the cart out.' 'Well, what's that then?'

MRS WELSH *enters unseen and watches.*

'I was going to the bakery.' 'Oh really, Mr Peck?' 'Oh yes, Mrs Welsh.' 'Why are you getting the cart out to go two hundred yards to the bakery? How many buns were you intending to buy?' 'But Miss Addison said – '

CAROLYN *sits up from underneath the blanket to protest.*

CAROLYN. Mr Peck!

She sees MRS WELSH *and is frozen.* MR PECK *hasn't seen her.*

MR PECK. 'Put the cart away, Mr Peck.' 'Yes, Mrs Welsh.' 'Oh Miss Addison, what a delightful surprise!'

MR PECK *turns round and sees* MRS WELSH.

Bloody hell.

CAROLYN. For God's sake, Mr Peck!

MRS WELSH. Do I really sound like that? Don't answer. Thank you, Mr Peck, that'll be all.

MR PECK. Ma'am. (*Exits.*)

MRS WELSH. What do you think you were doing? (*Spotting the leaflet in her hand.*) What's that? Hand it over.

CAROLYN *hands over a flyer for the suffrage rally.*

You know perfectly well that this sort of bluster has no place here. Did Miss Blake give you this?

CAROLYN. Well… .

MRS WELSH. Did she? She did, didn't she.

CAROLYN. Ma'am – she only suggested we might be interested. She didn't force us, she told us not to tell – I mean – she told us… I wanted to go; she won't get into trouble, will she?

MISS BLAKE *enters*.

MISS BLAKE. Ah, Mrs Welsh, I was hoping to catch you…

MRS WELSH. Go to your room, Carolyn.

CAROLYN *goes*.

MISS BLAKE. Is everything alright?

MRS WELSH (*holding up the leaflet*). What's this?

MISS BLAKE. Oh. Mrs Welsh –

MRS WELSH. You know my stance on this.

MISS BLAKE. I don't see the harm in inviting the girls to listen.

MRS WELSH. If we get blown off-course at all, now –

MISS BLAKE. I don't believe this. We've already told them they can't speak, now they can't listen!

MRS WELSH. Their right to graduate hangs in the balance.

MISS BLAKE. What about their right to vote for who runs the country? For their future! Surely that's more important.

MRS WELSH. No, it is not.

Beat.

MISS BLAKE. You can't possible mean that. (*Beat.*) It's just a meeting.

Beat.

MRS WELSH. Miss Blake. You're going to have to make a decision.

MISS BLAKE. Please. Please don't ask me to choose.

A stand-off.

Scene Five

Outcasts

Night-time. TESS *is sitting reading a book.* CELIA *arrives, looking for her.*

CELIA. What are you doing out here?

TESS. Daydreaming.

CELIA. It's the middle of the night. Listen, have you finished your Cuvier notes? Caro thinks we need to learn the fossil studies. Have you read them?

She takes the half-finished poem out of TESS' *hand.*

TESS. Give it back! It's impossible. Nothing rhymes with orchard.

CELIA. Pilchard.

TESS. What?

CELIA. Pilchard rhymes with orchard. Sort of. Use that.

TESS. You can't write a love poem about a pilchard.

CELIA. You could. 'A pilchard caught swimming off Dover...'

TESS. Alright! I'll do Cuvier later.

CELIA. The test's tomorrow.

TESS. I can't concentrate.

CELIA. Just think about something else. Cuvier. How was botany?

Beat.

Tess?

TESS. I'm thinking. About Cuvier.

CELIA. Tess, don't –

TESS. Just leave me be.

CELIA. You can't risk another failure.

TESS. I haven't failed anything.

CELIA. Carolyn told me.

TESS. What?

CELIA. About botany.

TESS. She's got no business –

CELIA. I said I'd help you.

TESS. I don't want your help.

CELIA. You need it.

TESS. I don't. If I do, I'll ask for it.

CELIA. You're too proud, Tess.

TESS. You're just jealous.

CELIA. What?

TESS. Of what I've got with Ralph.

CELIA. I worked hard to get here, I'm not about to throw it away.

TESS. I'm not throwing it away.

CELIA. He'll ruin your education –

TESS. He is an education.

CELIA. He's not.

TESS. I'm just not interested in Cuvier! And today, three hours on the science of war? I don't see the point.

CELIA. It means we won't make the same mistakes again.

TESS. Who?

CELIA. Us. People.

TESS. No, Celia. Men. It means men won't make the same mistakes again. The only impact we women ever had on war was when Brudenell's wife knitted him a new jersey and the troops said, 'That looks warm, what do you call that, Lord *Cardigan*?' We don't get to make decisions –

CELIA. We do.

TESS. Like what?

CELIA. Like family. Don't you want to teach your children to be good, responsible people?

TESS. Oh, that's exactly what we need, another lot of good, responsible, quiet women while our sons stand up in Parliament.

CELIA. And you're going to change that how? By giving up!

TESS. We can't compete, we can't even vote.

CELIA. And we'll never get the vote if you sit under an apple tree all night.

TESS. At least in an orchard I know where I am.

Beat.

CELIA. What's happened to you? You used to want this so much. He's put doubts in your head, hasn't he?

TESS. What?

CELIA. He doesn't approve.

TESS. You don't know him. He's not like the others.

CELIA. They hate us being here.

TESS. He believes in this! Maybe more than I do. It's me, Celia. I just don't know what I want any more.

CELIA. Listen. If he believes in this, then he likes you because of your mind. We're thinkers, scientists!

TESS. Outcasts.

CELIA. What?

TESS. We're bluestockings, Celia. Untouchables. If I mess this up with Ralph then who else is going to have me? We're not good Christian women any more. We're not meek and mild. We're dissenters. No one will have us. What if I want to be a mother? It's all very well for you.

CELIA. What's that supposed to mean?

TESS. You've never had a – you only want… You know what I mean.

CELIA. I only want what?

Pause. CELIA *is hurt.*

You really have no idea, do you.

TESS. Come on.

CELIA. You should watch yourself, Tess. I've never – I haven't – I mean, I've never had a Ralph. I want that too. Almost more than anything. But being here… it's not until it's taken away that you understand. They sent me home. Nervous exhaustion. I worked through till dawn every night then went straight to prayers. I had to fight to come back. What would I have done if they'd said no? Don't throw this away. Not when it's only just started.

Scene Six

Raising the Banner

CAROLYN *and* TESS *are in* MRS LINDLEY*'s haberdashery buying fabric for a banner. The doorbell rings and* LLOYD *and* EDWARDS *enter.*

EDWARDS. Hello, ladies.

MRS LINDLEY. Gentlemen. I was about to close.

While they talk, MRS LINDLEY *cuts the fabric to size and measures out the ribbon for the* WOMEN.

LLOYD. Oh, we can wait.

EDWARDS. Hello, ladies. Is that for a dress for Newmarket?

CAROLYN. Not unless I'm to troop around the paddock in forty yards of calico.

LLOYD. We haven't seen you around much.

EDWARDS. I was hoping we'd see you more often.

TESS. Well. We mostly take lectures at college now.

CAROLYN. Maudsley had us banned.

LLOYD. We know. We heard.

CAROLYN. Will it take paint, the calico?

MRS LINDLEY. What sort of paint?

CAROLYN. Just something – for lettering. Emulsion.

MRS LINDLEY. Yes, it'll take paint.

LLOYD. Do you think a banner's going to help? Are you really intending to fight this?

MRS LINDLEY *packages the fabric*. HOLMES *arrives*.

HOLMES. Ladies. Fellas, what are you doing here?

LLOYD. Just seeing what's on display.

MRS LINDLEY. Mr Holmes. Your package arrived from Paris this morning.

HOLMES. Good, thank you. And do you approve?

MRS LINDLEY. Silk brocade with double stitching? Absolutely.

She opens a box containing a delicate pair of gloves.

HOLMES. Let's have a look. Well, ladies, what do you think?

CAROLYN. Maison Worth? They're all the rage on the Champs-Elysées.

HOLMES. They're this season's. Thank you, ma'am. Fellas, see you back at college.

LLOYD (*suddenly*). You can't seriously believe you'll win?

CAROLYN. We might do.

HOLMES. But, ladies, you can't vote.

CAROLYN. Nor can you.

LLOYD. We can't, no, but all of the graduates can. I'm afraid there's little point in your motion.

HOLMES. Lloyd. That's enough.

MRS LINDLEY. That's three and six.

TESS (*paying and making to leave*). Thank you. Carolyn, let's / go.

LLOYD. What would you do with a degree anyway? Run the country? Be an engineer? Develop a cure for smallpox?

CAROLYN. Maybe. I'm going to be a doctor.

LLOYD. And who are you going to doctor, miss? Me? Him? No? Who?

HOLMES. Alright, Lloyd, that's enough.

LLOYD (*to* CAROLYN). Who?!

CAROLYN. Just because you don't believe a woman capable of –

LLOYD. No man will be doctored by a woman.

TESS. Plenty of women will.

LLOYD. But no man will employ you. No man will take your directions. No man will vote for you. So you're a lost cause. Why fight it?

CAROLYN. Because / it's who –

LLOYD (*explodes suddenly*). Listen! I was at school at five. At seven I knew Plato. At twelve, hand me a cadaver and I'd tell you the name of every last nerve in it. You think you can compete? You think some tuppenny once-a-week governess is enough, do you? Some tattered notes from your brother? Some village dunce school for girls? You think *that* – that joke of an education – gives you a right to set foot here? At Cambridge? Cambridge, for God's sake! This isn't some country-hole second-rate pauper's college. We're not average men here. We are the future. The leaders. The establishment. We don't sleep, we don't rest, we don't give up and we don't come second. We learn. It's our right. It's our blood. And we stop at nothing. These buildings. They make us men. Eight hundred years we've studied here. We built this country. We made this nation. Darwin, Milton,

Shadwell, Marlowe, Gladstone, Newton, Cromwell, Pitt. Then you. You what? Waltz in, with your bonnets and your pretentions and your preposterous self-belief and think you have a right to set foot in these walls? To put yourself on a level with us because you can heat a test tube on a burner? You know what they should do with you – they should put you away. You're mad. You're not natural. You don't have an ounce of womanhood in your body. You won't be mothers. And you won't be wives. Why would you do that? No normal woman would want that. Cos you know no man'll ever have you. You're a joke. All of you. A joke! Ha, a doctor, for God's sake!

CAROLYN. I know the human body as well as any man.

LLOYD. Well, I'll be damned if any man would let you touch his body unless he's paying you like a common whore.

The WOMEN *stand for a moment in stunned silence and then leave. A pause.*

HOLMES. That was harsh, Lloyd.

LLOYD. They're going to lose anyway, they might as well get used to it. Now, if you'd be so kind, we're after some ladies' stockings. Just one pair. Blue stockings. Any size.

MRS LINDLEY. Get out.

LLOYD. What did you say?

MRS LINDLEY. Get out of my shop.

LLOYD. Well! My father will be disappointed to hear one of his establishments is being lorded over by a bluestocking supporter. And what with the numbers of bids for the leases pouring in…

LLOYD *goes to leave.*

MRS LINDLEY. Alright. Here. A pair of blue stockings. Take them.

LLOYD *pushes a note across the counter.*

LLOYD. Thanks. (*Pointedly.*) Keep the change.

Scene Seven

An Emergency Summit

MISS BLAKE *is waiting for* MR BANKS *in a tea parlour. Others are seated nearby.* MR BANKS *arrives looking flustered.*

MR BANKS. I'm so late, I know, I'm sorry. Flat tyre.

MISS BLAKE. Confounded by your own laws of motion?

MR BANKS. Yes, thank you.

MISS BLAKE. Why didn't you get a taxi?

MR BANKS (*avoiding the question*). Have you ordered tea?

MISS BLAKE. Not yet –

MR BANKS. It can wait. Why don't we...

He steers her away from the proximity of other tables.

Look, we're in trouble.

MISS BLAKE. What's going on?

MR BANKS. The opposition are gathering strength.

MISS BLAKE. So are we.

MR BANKS. Not on this scale. They've laid on extra trains. Every hotel for thirty miles is booked out. We won't stand a chance.

MISS BLAKE. We have a good number of supporters.

MR BANKS. The graduates are coming up from London, they're not going to listen to us.

MISS BLAKE. There must be a way –

MR BANKS. Well, I don't know it.

MISS BLAKE. Is there no one you can talk to?

MR BANKS. I'm powerless. I'm a traitor.

MISS BLAKE. There must be something. Thomas, this is all we have. I arrived at Girton at eighteen and never left. I'll never be a mother. To be a woman and know... At least you have a family; you have Rose and the girls, and you have Trinity.

MR BANKS. Trinity sacked me.

MISS BLAKE. What?! Thomas, I don't believe it.

MR BANKS. When they found out I was involved with the vote, they withdrew the offer, filled my old position with one of my own students – and now my wife won't even look at me since we can't even afford a fish on a Friday.

MISS BLAKE. Why didn't you tell me?

MR BANKS. I'm sorry, it just didn't seem real.

MISS BLAKE. So we focus on this. Come on, Thomas.

MR BANKS. And if we lose?

MISS BLAKE. The suffragists are making a stand in Market Square. They're gathering supporters for voting day.

MR BANKS. Don't bring them into it.

MISS BLAKE. They're a powerful ally.

MR BANKS. Elizabeth won't allow it.

MISS BLAKE. Elizabeth won't know.

MR BANKS. If you go behind her back – you could be sidelined, even dismissed.

MISS BLAKE. I couldn't. I've resigned.

Beat.

Thomas, I'm leaving.

The emotion suddenly hits her and she wells up.

MR BANKS. Eleanor!

MISS BLAKE. I'm sorry. (*Gathers herself together.*) She couldn't see past the campaigning.

MR BANKS. Eleanor, you can't leave. What'll you do? Where will you go?

MISS BLAKE. I don't know. Girton's all I have.

MR BANKS. Go and see her, for God's sake, tell her you've changed your mind.

MISS BLAKE. It is too late. She forced my hand.

The WAITER *reappears. They return to their table, downtrodden.*

WAITER. Will it be the usual for the two of you, sir?

MR BANKS. I think perhaps just tea. Thanks.

WAITER. Nothing else at all. Right you are then. (*Pause. Quietly.*) Let me see what I can get on the house.

MR BANKS. Thank you.

A couple leave the next table. The LADY *stops at their table on her way past and speaks to* MISS BLAKE.

LADY. I heard what you were saying. About the vote and ladies' rights.

MR BANKS (*to* MISS BLAKE). You see! A kindred spirit.

LADY. You should be ashamed of yourself. Have you no sense of propriety and womanly feeling? Frank, we're leaving. I do hope you lose.

She walks out. Her HUSBAND *nods at them with a sense of awkward politeness.*

Scene Eight

King of Hearts

*That evening in the JCR at Trinity College. RALPH and a
group of friends are having a rowdy time. HOLMES is shuffling
the cards. LLOYD is pouring brandies. WILL appears; he is
looking for RALPH. EDWARDS is tipsy.*

HOLMES. Bennett! What brings you here?

WILL. I'm looking for Ralph / Mayhew.

EDWARDS. Bennett's here!

HOLMES. Do you want in? We're about to kick off.

WILL. Is Ralph Mayhew here?

HOLMES. Mayhew! Visitor.

EDWARDS. Mayhew…

RALPH. Hey, d'you want to join us? Pick three cards. Here you
are.

WILL. Oh, right. Thanks!

He picks some cards.

RALPH. You're not a Trinity fellow, are you? You're in Banks's
natural science class.

WILL. That's right.

RALPH. Can I get you a brandy?

EDWARDS. Brandy!

WILL. I'd better not.

EDWARDS. He'd better not.

RALPH. Come on, just a sniff?

WILL. If you insist.

HOLMES. Edwards, these are your cards.

EDWARDS. Why can't I pick them myself?

RALPH. What can I do for you?

WILL. I wanted to talk to you about – I have a friend, you know her well, I think, she's at –

LLOYD. And the losing suits is – (*Picking a card.*) Spades!

RALPH. Hold that thought – let's talk afterwards. Have you played before?

WILL. No.

RALPH. Simple enough. Spades you lose, pull a King and you win. Are you ready?

They take it in turns to put a card down from the three they've picked. It's fast. Each time they lay a card, they're safe unless it's a Spade, in which case they have to drink. Anyone who pulls a King wins the game. They get excited whenever there's a face card.

HOLMES. I'll draw first. Clubs, ten.

LLOYD. Hearts, four.

RALPH. Diamonds, six.

WILL. Clubs, three.

EDWARDS. I don't believe this. Spades, two.

LLOYD. Drink!

HOLMES. Come on, all of it! Down the hatch!

EDWARDS finishes his glass and puts it upside down on his head to prove it's empty. It's refilled.

Lloyd, you draw.

LLOYD. Diamonds, eight.

RALPH. Clubs, Jack.

WILL. Hearts, three.

EDWARDS. Oh Jesus. Spades, eight. You've rigged it!

HOLMES. Don't be ridiculous.

RALPH. Come on, Edwards, it's still half-empty!

EDWARDS *finishes his second drink, to cheers. It's refilled.*

HOLMES. Clubs, five. Final round. Will, why don't you start?

WILL. Alright. Diamonds, Queen.

LLOYD. I'm Clubs, nine.

HOLMES. Edwards.

EDWARDS *looks at his card but won't show it.*

Edwards!

RALPH. He's got Spades again, I don't believe it.

EDWARDS. Someone else go. Please!

LLOYD. Come on, show us your card.

EDWARDS (*showing his card*). Six of spades.

A roar. They all hoist EDWARDS *onto the table.* LLOYD *brandishes the bottle.*

LLOYD. Three in a row! Finish the bottle.

EDWARDS. That's not in the rules.

LLOYD. We made the rules.

EDWARDS. I'm completely skewered.

LLOYD. The bottle or a song.

EDWARDS. I'm almost dead!

Cheers of encouragement. EDWARDS *suddenly starts to sing. He sings it beautifully; the others didn't expect this. He sings a verse of 'The Last Rose of Summer' by Thomas Moore.*

''Tis the last rose of summer, left blooming alone,
All her lovely companions are faded and gone.
No flowers of her kindred, no rosebud is nigh,
To reflect back her blushes and give sigh for sigh.'

The MEN *stand in shock. Then they start to clap and cheer.*

EDWARDS *then downs his glass and puts it upside down on his head.*

HOLMES. Come on, we still haven't finished. Clubs, six.

RALPH. Hearts – King! Look at that, and I win!

LLOYD. King of Hearts!

HOLMES. King of Hearts? You're not far off that.

RALPH. Bugger off. I'm a changed man, I tell you. I've been blessed by Venus.

EDWARDS. Bacchus more like.

RALPH. Bugger off, Edwards.

EDWARDS. Bugger off, Edwards.

They all toast raucously.

HOLMES. Who is she?

RALPH. I'm serious.

LLOYD. Mayhew's going to make a speech.

EDWARDS. Hurrah!

RALPH. No I'm not.

Uproar in protest. RALPH *happily gives in and stands on a table.*

Fellas! Gentlemen. I am in love.

LLOYD (*sings*). 'Whoa, there'll be a hot time in the old town tonight, my baby…'

RALPH. I'm serious! This is real. I hardly know what to do with myself. I can't eat, I can't sleep.

HOLMES. He can drink though!

There is a rally of voices and approval as RALPH *stands on a chair to make a toast.*

RALPH. Indeed I can. Gentlemen, I hope one day you shall all be as happy as I am.

Ripples of sarcasm from around the room.

She is glorious! And – you'll never believe it – she's not just a pretty face; though, fellas, you should see her face –

Whoops of disbelief and humour.

No, no. (*Rallies their attention.*) She is a wit. A bluestocking!

LLOYD. You must be mad.

HOLMES. Ralph, you're asking for trouble.

RALPH. Listen, you can think what you like. I don't care. I love her.

EDWARDS. He's in love.

RALPH. And I'll prove it to you. Look at this.

He produces a box from his pocket and opens it to shows them the ring.

Look.

LLOYD. Bloody hell.

EDWARDS. He's not kidding.

HOLMES. Where did you get it?

EDWARDS. Let me see.

He sobers up looking at it.

Sweet Jesus, Ralph! It's a trapiche emerald. Columbian. Look! Dark carbon.

RALPH. I had to pawn half I own to pay for it, but look at it. Perfection.

WILL. When are you going to ask her?

RALPH. Got to ask her father first, haven't I. I've not met him yet.

HOLMES. Always the gent.

RALPH. Thank you, sir.

EDWARDS. A toast, a toast!

RALPH. Friends. Let us raise our glasses. I should like to christen this term, the Newnham Dawn.

EDWARDS. The Newnham Dawn!

HOLMES. She's a Newnham girl?

RALPH. Yes, she is.

HOLMES. What's her name?

RALPH. Eliza. She's everything.

HOLMES. What happened to Tess?

RALPH. Tess was – wonderful. Wonderful.

LLOYD. But Girton's such a trek!

HOLMES. I'll drink to that. No more of the Girton grind.

RALPH. No more. Here's to Newnham ladies, bluestockings and all!

Cheers. WILL *stands apart, unable to speak.*

You got a girl, Will?

WILL. Me. No. I haven't.

RALPH. Fella, you don't look well. You're not a brandy drinker?

WILL. Not really. No.

RALPH. Let's get you outside.

He slaps him on the back and takes him out.

You alright, sir? Do you want a walk home?

WILL. No… I was looking out for Tess. I promised her father.

RALPH. Oh. Christ. Tess? I didn't know you knew her.

WILL. You haven't told her, have you.

RALPH. Look –

WILL. Have you.

RALPH. No. Look, I'm sorry. My father has expectations. Plans for me. And you can't argue with the man. Girton is – well, it's political. I tried to broach it with him but he was adamant, you know what it's like.

WILL. No. I don't know what it's like. Jesus. Newnham? How is that any different? It's a ladies' college, just like Girton.

RALPH. But it's not radical, it's respectable, they're not involved with all this stuff, graduation rights. Listen, I'm a scientist, I wasn't cut out to be a politician. I didn't want this. I didn't choose it. If you see her, will you wish her well.

RALPH *heads back in.* WILL *leaves.*

Scene Nine

Broken Hearts

A short while later. TESS *is on the bench in the orchard.* WILL *arrives.*

WILL. What are you doing in the orchard? It's the middle of the night, won't you get into trouble?

TESS. Only if Miss Bott finds me. Here, I've got cocoa from Paris. Do you want some?

He sits down next to her to share her cocoa.

WILL. Thank you. (*Pause.*) Tess…

TESS. I *was* revising.

WILL. I didn't say anything!

TESS. Will, I can take care of myself.

WILL. I know. I do trust you. I just don't trust a man you met in the street to –

TESS. We met in the library.

UNIVERSITY OF WINCHESTER
LIBRARY

WILL. Of course, how could I forget.

TESS. You offered to talk to him. If you'd talked to him you'd understand. You have lectures with him, it'd hardly be a hassle, but you refuse –

WILL. I didn't refuse.

TESS. So go!

WILL. I have. I've been. I've talked to him.

TESS. What? Will! Why didn't you say!

WILL. I've been trying. You wouldn't let me get a word in.

TESS. Thank you. Thank you!

She hugs him. He tries to unclasp her.

WILL. Tess, listen –

TESS. When? When did you talk to him?

WILL. Tonight.

TESS. How is he?

WILL. Tess –

TESS. What did he say? Did he ask to meet Father? Come on, what did he say?

WILL. Tess, I'm sorry. He's not suitable. He's not right for you.

Pause. TESS *can't believe this.*

TESS. He's not 'right for me'?!

WILL. Listen –

TESS. You're judging him? Based on what? His expansive mind? His predicated first! Are you serious? This is a joke, you've set this up, Celia's put you up to this because she doesn't approve.

WILL. Tess!

TESS. What!

WILL. I am serious, please! Just listen –

TESS. No, Will, no! You always do this, you and Father. I want to study, you try and stop me, I fall in love, you try and stop me. Why can't you just let me be me? This is what I want.

WILL. There's someone else.

TESS. Why is that so hard for you?

WILL. Tess! There's someone else.

Pause.

TESS. What?

WILL. Another girl.

Pause.

TESS. You're lying. You're making this up.

WILL. I'm not. I'm sorry.

TESS. You don't approve so you're making this up. (*In a daze of disbelief and denial.*) I've got to go inside, let me go in,

WILL. Tess –

TESS. I haven't finished my / work.

WILL. I heard him say.

TESS. I've got to finish my / work.

WILL. I saw the ring. I saw it. I'm sorry.

TESS *looks at him, heartbroken, not knowing what to do.* CELIA *arrives.*

I'm sorry, Tess.

CELIA. Tess? What's going on? Tess? Miss Bott's on the prowl. (*To* WILL.) You'd better shift yourself, quick.

WILL. I don't want to leave her. Tess?

CELIA. It's alright, I'll take her in. Quick!

WILL. Thank you. Tess. I'm sorry.

TESS *can't move. She's in shock.* WILL *leaves.* TESS *is broken.*

CELIA. What happened? What happened?

TESS. I've got to go in, I've got to pack.

CELIA. Pack? Tess!

TESS. I can't stay here, I can't be here. I have to go.

CELIA. Tess! Listen, I know I'm the last person you want to speak to, but don't do this.

TESS. I can't do it, I can't be here. I can't be here!

CELIA. Not now. Not when we're so close. Please!

TESS *heads to go inside,* CELIA *blocks her way and they almost struggle.*

Stop it. Stop it! What are you doing, you've worked so hard! Talk to me.

TESS *stops.*

TESS. There was a girl at home. Lived at the parsonage. Annabel. She'd spend a whole afternoon sewing a ribbon onto a bonnet, and she'd be content. Why wasn't that enough for me, Celia? You know, I'd climb the roof of Will's classroom just to listen. Once I lost my footing and they found me hanging by my underskirt, but I wouldn't let go of my notebook. I should have fallen and cracked my skull right then and there, I'd have been better off.

But no. I was stubborn. Forfeit any hope of reputation, of a good match, wreck Mother's nerves with worry, all for this, to be here. And then I meet a boy. A poet. A poet! In a library. And I fall for him like a rock. And suddenly I can't think because my mind is full of him. I read Keats and hear his voice. I look at Vermeer and there he is, in oils. And I love him with every thought and bone and sinew. And then he buys a ring. But it's not for me. And now. What am I now? He's caved out my heart, Celia. What do I do?

CELIA. You carry on.

TESS. I can't. I've got nothing left.

CELIA. That girl on the roof. What would she say to that? If she knew when you were grown, that you'd be standing here, now, ready to go home? You owe her more than that. We might graduate, Tess. Can't you see? We'd be the first. The first! Thank God we're not like Annabel. We're not passengers. People like us don't get buffeted by the wind; we change its course. We are the luckiest, luckiest women alive. And you're ready to pack up and go home? You do what you have to, but if you leave now you might as well have cracked your skull because that little girl would never forgive you. And nor would I. Come on. Tess?

Scene Ten

The Viva

COLLINS *and* RADLEIGH *enter with* MRS WELSH *to give the* WOMEN *their vivas.* CAROLYN, CELIA *and* TESS *stand.* TESS *is still weak from the stresses of the night before.*

COLLINS. Morning.

CAROLYN. Good morning.

COLLINS. I trust you are ready?

RADLEIGH. I hope you're not about to waste our time.

CELIA. No, sir.

COLLINS. Willbond, Addison and Moffat, yes?

MRS WELSH. That is correct.

COLLINS. Miss Willbond, I've read your papers. All eight hundred pages of them. You suggest here that a student in Zurich is legitimately challenging Galileo.

RADLEIGH. The man's seventeen.

COLLINS. You've read his thesis?

CELIA. All of it, sir.

COLLINS. You think Galileo got it wrong?

CELIA. Sir, he doesn't account for the constant speed of light; he assumed it was affected by where you are and how fast you're moving.

COLLINS. And now this Einstein has set his sights on Newton, we hear.

CELIA. I think he might be right to do so, sir.

COLLINS. Your evidence?

CELIA. Take the rotation of Mercury. The precession of the perihelion deviates from Newton's predictions.

COLLINS. Only slightly.

CELIA. By thirty-eight arc seconds per tropic century.

RADLEIGH. That's negligible.

CELIA. Absolutely. But it's enough to disprove a law. I think Mr Einstein may be quite ahead of his time.

COLLINS. Well, we shall see.

RADLEIGH. Miss Addison.

CAROLYN. Sir.

RADLEIGH. Maritime science. You propose, against common understanding, that icebergs don't always drift with the prevailing wind.

CAROLYN. Sir, there's often a drift angle of twenty to forty degrees to the right of the wind current.

RADLEIGH. And you know this how?

CAROLYN. I studied the charts from the *Fram*.

COLLINS. And if the iceberg rotates, how do you account for that?

CAROLYN. The only accurate way is to balance the frictional effects of the ocean current with the known Coriolis force, so they rotate –

COLLINS. – On an orbital path. Indeed. And you could balance this yourself?

CAROLYN. Yes, sir.

RADLEIGH. How?

CAROLYN. By getting on a boat and going out there, into the Atlantic.

COLLINS (*smiles*). This research is expensive. Could you justify it?

CAROLYN. Absolutely. The safety of Atlantic crossings might depend on it.

RADLEIGH. Miss Moffat. The classification of stars. You know the Draper Catalogue is generally regarded as groundbreaking?

TESS. It is, sir, without doubt, but I believe it could be improved.

COLLINS. How so?

TESS. By subdividing the stars according to temperature.

RADLEIGH. You want to measure the temperature of a star?

TESS. Yes, sir.

COLLINS. And how would you propose to do that?

TESS. By working out the ionisation of the photosphere.

COLLINS. But you don't have the telescopic equipment.

TESS. I wouldn't rely on telescopes, sir. If you split a star's light emissions with a diffraction grating, you can subdivide the photons into a spectrum and analyse the absorption lines.

RADLEIGH. Which tell you what?

TESS. Which ions are present in which chemical element.

COLLINS. Giving you the chemical composition of the photosphere –

TESS. And therefore the temperature.

Beat. She's on to something.

RADLEIGH. You've completed the practical study?

TESS. Not yet, sir.

RADLEIGH. Why not?

TESS. To do so I'd have to be in the Southern Hemisphere.

Beat.

RADLEIGH. Evolutionary theory. You cover Lamarck here but what of his opponents?

TESS. His opponents?

RADLEIGH. Cuvier.

Silence. TESS *is frozen. She then looks at* CELIA, *who knows she hasn't revised this subject.*

COLLINS. How does Cuvier critique the theory of spontaneous generation?

Silence. COLLINS *tries to assist her.*

What did he say about fossil records?

TESS. He noticed that sometimes new fossils appear as if out of nowhere.

RADLEIGH. For instance?

TESS. If a natural disaster wipes out a species, other organisms move in to replace them.

RADLEIGH. For example?

TESS. In a volcanic winter. There's increased sulphates in the soil, so it's more fertile…

COLLINS. Can you be more specific?

TESS. Ferns? Bacteria.

RADLEIGH. Name the arthropods in Cuvier's study.

Pause.

TESS. I… I don't remember.

RADLEIGH. Sorry?

TESS. I don't remember.

COLLINS. Tell me, where did he conduct his survey?

TESS. I think… Spain. No, France. France.

RADLEIGH. And the name of the process?

TESS. Strato… stratigraphy.

RADLEIGH. What type of stratigraphy?

TESS. Geostratigraphy.

RADLEIGH. Biostratigraphy.

COLLINS. With whom did he complete his study?

TESS. I'm sorry?

COLLINS. I just need the name of the scientist, Miss Moffat. The scientist and the year, please.

TESS. I'm sorry. I'm sorry, I don't remember. I don't know.

The tutors exchange looks. They return to their papers.

RADLEIGH. Miss Willbond. You're very thorough. I suggest you learn to be more succinct. You've passed. Well done.

COLLINS. Miss Addison, your self-assurance doesn't become you. Yet there's merit enough here to warrant a pass. Congratulations.

RADLEIGH. Miss Moffat. (*Holding her astronomy papers.*) These are quite remarkable. I am impressed. A pass requires excellence across the board, without exception. I'm afraid it's a fail.

COLLINS. Do persevere with astronomy in your own time, won't you. You have quite a talent. Mrs Welsh, ladies, thank you very much.

RADLEIGH *and* COLLINS *start to pack up.* TESS *is broken-hearted.*

TESS. What'll I do?

MRS WELSH. You'll go home.

CAROLYN. She can't go home!

MRS WELSH. Home has its merits. You can take long walks. See friends. Read. Spend time with your family. Recover your health.

TESS *turns away and fights back tears.*

Try to put Girton out of your mind.

TESS. I can't!

MRS WELSH. But you must.

A pause. TESS *takes in the enormity of the situation.* MRS WELSH *gathers herself, then –*

Then, when your health returns, you will pack your trunk, get back on the train and make sure you're not late for the beginning of term in September.

TESS. What? But Mrs Welsh…!

COLLINS *and* RADLEIGH *watch all of this.*

MRS WELSH. Occasionally, just occasionally, it is right to make an exception to a rule. Though don't think you're getting off lightly. You will be resitting.

TESS. Of course, ma'am. I won't let you down. I promise.

COLLINS *can't help smiling. The* WOMEN *celebrate. Music swells and the large banner is hoisted up… it is voting day, jubilation!*

Scene Eleven

Voting Day

The room is now strung with banners and decorations for voting day and the WOMEN *are in high spirits. Two large banner hangs aloft, reading 'Degrees for Women' and 'Gowns for Girtonites'.* MRS WELSH *is speaking to the assembled students.*

MRS WELSH. If the vote goes our way, just think, amongst you now may stand the first female Cambridge graduates. The first! What an honour. You have certainly proved yourselves worthy candidates.

But if the voters aren't kind, we mustn't be dispirited. A certificate is merely ink on a page. No one can take away your knowledge. Yet one can't help but hope. Let's put our faith in the voters and pray.

Pause.

CELIA. I hate this waiting, I hate it.

MRS WELSH. We've always had to wait. We waited eight hundred years for a college. I think, in the scheme of things, another half an hour won't hurt.

TESS. They're voting right now. (*Pause.*) This very moment some man is putting a cross in a box. A man who's never met us.

MRS WELSH. He's there... and we're here.

Pause.

CAROLYN. When I lived in Burundi –

TESS. Here we go.

CAROLYN. When I lived in Burundi, the villagers chose their chief by putting stones in a pot. And I was allowed a stone. We all lived there, so we all had a stone. In Burundi. (*Pause.*) I'm just saying.

WILL *enters with* MINNIE, *he is flustered.*

TESS. Will!

MRS WELSH. Is there any news?

WILL. I don't know, ma'am, but I think the gates should be shut.

MRS WELSH. What are you talking about?

MR BANKS. Is everything alright?

WILL. People are rather up in arms.

MRS WELSH. I'm sure it's just some overzealous students.

WILL. It's not. With respect, ma'am, there's men on the streets. Train-loads of them.

MRS WELSH. Perhaps we ought to keep our festivities indoors. Although it's a shame / to –

WILL. You're not listening, ma'am. It's bedlam out there.

Pause.

MRS WELSH. Minnie, fetch my coat.

MINNIE. Yes, ma'am. (*Exits.*)

WILL. It's no business for a lady.

MRS WELSH. If it's anyone's business, it's mine. Now please –

MR BANKS. Elizabeth, let me go.

MRS WELSH. No. You hold the fort. I will go.

WILL. Mrs Welsh. I beg you, it's not safe.

MRS WELSH. Don't be absurd.

MR BANKS. What's going on?

WILL. It's chaos, sir. They've broken windows. Pulled down the theatre hoardings and the railings from Queens' and set them on fire in the square. The police can't get near them. And they were heading this way.

MR BANKS. Lord knows what they'll do when they get here.

WILL. It's too dangerous. You should get out of here, all of you. Just go, go out the back way. Don't, for God's sake, go near them.

MRS WELSH. This is preposterous. I've worked my whole life for this day and I refuse to have it compromised by some petulant juveniles. They have no right! (*Goes to exit.*)

WILL. Not you. Please. Don't let her go, sir.

MRS WELSH. Don't tell me what to do. I will speak to them.

WILL. You don't understand! They've made an effigy – ma'am.

Beat.

MRS WELSH. What?

WILL. A woman on a bicycle, a plaque round its neck. They strung it up, paraded it like Guy Fawkes. A woman in blue stockings. And then, when they got to the square – when they got to the square they doused it in oil and burnt it. Stood and cheered and watched it burn.

Beat.

MR BANKS. Elizabeth –

MRS WELSH *puts her hand out to silence him. She is holding back tears but won't let herself crack.*

WILL. Anyone voting yes has been sought out. They chased them down, throwing rocks, firecrackers, anything they could lay their hands on. They're out of control, ma'am. There's thousands of them on the streets –

MRS WELSH. That's enough. Enough! Minnie! I'll get my coat myself. They shall not make a mockery of us. I'll be damned if they do.

She exits.

MR BANKS. Elizabeth!

He goes towards the exit.

TESS (*to* WILL). Are you alright?

WILL. No. You?

TESS. Not really.

WILL. Well then.

A window smashes. Sounds of protestors outside.

TESS. Jesus!

WILL. Mr Banks, get the girls out now, let me talk to them.

MR BANKS. But –

WILL. Now!

Another smash from somewhere else, off.

CELIA. No!

TESS. Celia!

Another smash and then the MEN *enter, a whole crowd, headed up by* LLOYD *and* HOLMES. *They stand in a line, unmoving, terrifying. Silence.*

HOLMES (*looking at the banners*). This isn't right. It can't be right.

LLOYD. To hell with that.

He goes for the banner.

MR BANKS. What do you think you are doing?

The MEN *pull the banner down.*

Get out.

Silence.

I don't think you heard me. I said get out. If you leave now, there'll be minimal trouble.

WILL. Fellas. Please. Just go home.

HOLMES. What the hell are you doing here?

WILL. I said go home. You shouldn't be here.

LLOYD. *You* shouldn't be here. You're not one of them, are you? (*Indicating* MR BANKS.) Like he is.

LLOYD *is rounding on* WILL.

TESS. Will, be careful!

LLOYD. Whose side are you on? You're with us or against us.

HOLMES. Lloyd. That's enough.

LLOYD. Whose side are you on?!

WILL. I'd be ashamed to be on yours.

LLOYD punches WILL and knocks him down.

TESS. Stop it! Stop it!

WILL launches himself back to LLOYD. It erupts.

MR BANKS. Get out!

One of the MEN punches MR BANKS, who is knocked to the floor. MRS WELSH has entered, unseen, and surveys the scene with horror.

MRS WELSH. What on earth!

Everything goes silent. As she speaks she slowly loses control as she gets more and more distressed, until she lurches at them. All her careful self-control bursts until she is like an animal.

Dear God. What have you done? How dare you? How dare you come in here like this? Thirty years we slave for this day – and you – You should be ashamed. It's a sin. Do you have no respect? No thought? No dignity? It's not your livelihood. You've sacrificed nothing. Nothing! We sweat. Bleed. We give up everything we have in the world for this and you… you're barbarians. Barbarians! Get out. Get out. All of you. Out! Out!

She rushes at LLOYD, who, in one fell swoop, throws her to the ground.

HOLMES. Lloyd!

She lies there, unmoving. They are all paralysed with shock. She stays on the floor. HOLMES goes to help her and she refuses. Very slowly she picks herself up. As she does, MR PECK enters from the opposite side and takes his hat off.

One by one they all notice him. MRS WELSH *still has her back turned but senses that he is there.*

MRS WELSH. Mr Peck. Is there any news?

Silence. He doesn't have the heart to say the words. She musters the courage to speak again.

Mr Peck. Is there news?!

MR PECK. I'm sorry, ma'am. We lost.

No one moves. There's a collective moment of everyone taking in the new reality. EDWARDS *helps* MR BANKS *to his feet.* WILL *and* TESS *remain frozen, standing side by side.* MR BANKS *has been in a daze.*

MR BANKS. We lost?

MRS WELSH. Yes, we lost. (*Silence.*) We lost.

She falters. MR BANKS *puts his arm round her, and takes her out.* LLOYD *and the crowd exit, leaving* EDWARDS, HOLMES *and* WILL.

EDWARDS (*gently*). So, what happens now?

TESS. What?

EDWARDS. What'll you do now? You girls?

TESS. What do you mean, what'll we do?

EDWARDS. Well, now… now it's all over. I mean, you won't stay, will you? If you can't graduate. What's the point?

WILL. Edwards.

HOLMES (*exploding*). No one wanted this! Not for it to get out of hand. Look at this place. It's a feat. Places like this don't happen without blood and sweat. Regardless of what we think, you don't deserve this. We built this country on revolution, didn't we? This country wasn't built by conformists. I can't agree with your campaign. I'm afraid I think the damage would outweigh any benefits for the ladies. But, by God, I respect you. And I won't see you dishonoured. Ladies, I'm sorry for your loss.

HOLMES *exits.*

EDWARDS. I didn't mean to be rude, really. I'm not saying you should leave. You should stay. If you want to. I'm just… what are you going to do? If your whole course, this place, if it's not recognised – any of it – it's like no one'll even know you were here. What will you do?

WILL. Tess? What will you do?

Pause. She takes them both in, looks to CELIA *and* CAROLYN, *then back to the* MEN.

TESS. We'll carry on. We'll carry on.

WILL. Good. Good. Thank God for that.

Scene Twelve

If You Had to Choose

WILL *is walking up the platform with his suitcase, ready to board the train. He is leaving for the summer. Then out of nowhere,* TESS *appears, out of breath.*

TESS. Wait! Will!

He doesn't hear her.

Will!!

WILL. Tess. What are you doing here?

TESS. Don't get on the train. Not yet.

WILL. What?

TESS. Please. I have to… (*Pause. Turns away, steeling herself.*) Oh God.

WILL. Tess? (*Pause.*) I do have a train…

TESS. 'What if you had to choose – between love and knowledge?' I was asked to choose. And I couldn't; I couldn't choose. But now, I know. I could never choose love.

Not alone, not over this. Learning, life. I'd never be happy, and nor would he. I can't be the woman who waits. I'm a scientist, I want to go to the Andes and chart the Southern Cross. I'd be a terrible wife!

WILL. Tess –

TESS. Please. I can't love again. Not wholly. Not yet. My heart hurts still and it's fragile and I'm scared. But in time. I hope…

WILL. I'll wait. I'm not going anywhere. Not without you.

Pause.

TESS. I'm going to Peru.

Pause.

WILL. And I'm getting on a train. But I'm coming back, in September. Are you?

TESS. Yes. I'll be here in September. I'm not going anywhere.

WILL. Good. Good!

They embrace. There is an anthem and a triumphant song. As they sing, the following script appears, either by projection or on three banners that they hoist down from above.

'The Girton girls continued to match their male peers grade for grade.

Eventually the Senate succumbed to pressure and Cambridge awarded women the right to graduate.

It was fifty years later, in 1948.'

UNIVERSITY OF WINCHESTER
LIBRARY

www.nickhernbooks.co.uk

facebook.com/nickhernbooks

twitter.com/nickhernbooks